Illustrator:
Agi Palinay

Editors:
Dona Herweck Rice
Janet Cain

Editorial Project Manager:
Evan D. Forbes, M.S. Ed.

Editor-in-Chief:
Sharon Coan, M.S. Ed.

Art Director:
Elayne Roberts

Cover Artist:
Karen Walstad

Product Manager:
Phil Garcia

Imaging:
Hillary Merriman

Publishers:
Rachelle Cracchiolo, M.S. Ed.
Mary Dupuy Smith, M.S. Ed.

EXTENDED THEMATIC UNIT

Celebrate Our
Similarities
Primary

Author:
Betty Burke

Teacher Created Materials, Inc.
P.O. Box 1040
Huntington Beach, CA 92647
ISBN-1-55734-508-2

©1995 Teacher Created Materials, Inc.
Made in U.S.A.

Table of Contents

Table of Contents (cont.)

Introduction

Celebrate Our Similarities contains a captivating, whole-language, extended thematic unit about the ways in which all people are the same. This unit has 176 exciting pages that are filled with a wide variety of lesson ideas and reproducible pages designed for use with primary students. The theme is connected to the curriculum with activities in reading, language arts (including written expression), science, social studies, math, art, music, physical education, and life skills. Many of these activities encourage cooperative learning.

Celebrate Our Similarities is divided into the following sections to allow for easy thematic planning: Everybody Eats Food, Everybody Wears Clothes, Everybody Needs a Place to Live, Everybody Communicates, Everybody Uses Transportation, Everybody Goes to School, Everybody Likes Stories, Everybody Has Games and Toys, Everybody Listens to Music, Everybody Creates with Arts and Crafts, Everybody Celebrates Special Days, and Everybody Needs a Friend.

This extended thematic unit includes:

- **Bulletin Board Ideas**—time-saving suggestions and plans for bulletin boards that are related to each section

- **Planning Guides**—suggestions for sequencing lessons for each section

- **Curriculum Connections**—relating the theme to language arts, math, science, social studies, art, music, physical education, and life skills

- **Suggested Literature**—summaries and activities that allow literature to be easily connected to the theme

- **Writing Ideas**—writing suggestions and activities that cross the curriculum

- **Group Projects**—to foster cooperative learning

- **Hands-On Activities**—providing opportunities for students to be active learners

- **Research Topics**—listing a variety of topics that can be used to extend and enrich learning

- **Bibliography**—suggesting additional books related to each section

- **Culminating Activities**—which require students to synthesize their learning and participate in activities that can be shared with others

---

To keep this valuable resource intact so that it can be used year after year, you may wish to punch holes in the pages and store them in a three-ring binder.

4

Introduction *(cont.)*

What Is Thematic Teaching?

Thematic teaching is a method of instruction that allows the teacher to establish an overall interesting idea or a sequence of interesting ideas to which all of the skills and concepts required by the curriculum can be related. Learning experiences need to relate to each other and to the needs and experiences of the children, as well as provide some perspective of the world outside the classroom. Thematic teaching allows for this.

Why an Extended Thematic Unit?

Themes can be as short as one day in length or last an entire school year. Although the duration of a theme is an individual choice, *Celebrate Our Similarities* has been designed to take you through an entire school year. How you use the extended theme in this book will depend greatly on your comfort level with thematic teaching.

Celebrate Our Similarities allows for in-depth study of some of the ways that people from around the world are the same. Since the theme is carried on throughout the year, students are given an opportunity to be immersed in the topic. A wide variety of activities is provided so you can easily meet the needs of your students. In addition, a bibliography is included to help you choose literature that will enrich your thematic unit. The culminating activities are designed so they can be done either as individual projects or combined into one celebration.

Why Whole Language?

A whole-language approach involves children in using all modes of communication: reading, writing, listening, observing, illustrating, experiencing, and doing. Communication skills are interconnected and integrated into lessons that emphasize the whole of language rather than isolating its parts. The lessons revolve around a selected theme. Reading is not taught as a separate subject from writing and spelling, for example. A child reads, writes, speaks, listens, and thinks in response to a specific theme introduced by the teacher. In this way, language skills grow naturally, stimulated by involvement and interest in the topic at hand.

Why Cooperative Learning?

Besides academic skills and content, students need to learn social skills. No longer can this area of development be taken for granted. Students must learn to work cooperatively in groups in order to function well in modern society. Group activities should be a regular part of school life and teachers should consciously include social objectives as well as academic objectives in their planning. The teacher should clarify and monitor the qualities of good group interaction, just as he/she would clarify and monitor the academic goals of the project.

Using a Multicultural Theme

Why Use a Multicultural Theme That Focuses on Similarities?

The goals of this extended thematic unit are the following:

1. To prepare students to live harmoniously in a multi-ethnic society
2. To help students recognize the importance of cooperation among the peoples of the world
3. To show students that people from around the world have the same basic needs, such as food, clothing, and shelter
4. To show students that people from around the world participate in many of the same types of activities, such as going to school, listening to music, reading stories, and creating things using arts and crafts
5. To promote positive self-images by providing students with the opportunity to share information about themselves

Explaining What Culture Is

When introducing the concept of what a culture is, explain that it is the way of life for a group of people. These people share many things, such as their history, language, beliefs, values, celebrations, art, music, literature, recipes, and the ways in which they do things. Many countries are represented by a variety of cultures that blend together while still retaining their individual identities.

Activities for Introducing *Celebrate Our Similarities*

1. Have students find magazine pictures of children from around the world. Ask them to work together to use the pictures to make a class collage on a bulletin board.
2. Have students ask family members from where their relatives originally came. Provide a wall map of the world and have students use colored map pins to mark those places on the map.

   Have students use the world map on page 173 to color the places that have colored pins on the wall map.
3. Read aloud the poem "Children, Children Everywhere" by Jack Prelutsky. Have students draw a picture to go with the poem. Then copy the poem on poster board and hang it on the wall. Display students' pictures around the poem.
4. Play a variety of folk music for students. Have them draw pictures of things they think of as they listen to the music.
5. Provide students with copies of the Greeting Cards on pages 7-10. Explain to students that these children are dressed in the traditional clothing of their cultures. Discuss the many ways to say "Hello" in the different languages. Have students color and cut out the cards. You may wish to have students glue the cards to make a multicultural folder for work that they do during this unit. An alternate suggestion is to have students work with a partner, combine their cards, and play concentration, using the cards. Have students practice greeting you in a different language each day. Try to greet them in a different language, too.
6. Read a variety of folk tales from different countries. A suggested list of folk tales is provided in the bibliography.
7. Have students learn to sing "It's a Small World" by Richard M. Sherman and Robert B. Sherman.

Greeting Cards

Directions: Color and cut apart the cards shown below. Learn how people from around the world say "Hello." Try saying "Hello" to your teacher, using a different language each day.

God dag from Sweden!

Bam dia from Brazil!

Aloha from Hawaii!

Jo reggelt from Hungary!

Continue working on page 8.

Greeting Cards *(cont.)*

Directions: Color and cut the cards shown below. Learn how other people from around the world say "Hello." Each day, try saying "Hello" to your teacher, using one of these languages.

Dobry den from Czechoslovakia!

Kahlee from Greece!

Doh-broh-yeh Oo-troh from Russia!

Konichiwa from Japan!

Continue working on page 9.

8

Greeting Cards *(cont.)*

Directions: Color and cut apart the cards shown below. Learn how some people from around the world say "Hello." Each day, try saying "Hello" to your teacher, using one of these languages.

Bon Jour from France!

Jambo from Kenya!

Ram-ram from India!

Guten Tag from Germany

Continue working on page 10.

Greeting Cards *(cont.)*

Directions: Color and cut apart the cards shown below. Learn how more people from around the world say "Hello." Try saying "Hello" to your teacher, using a different language each day. On the last card, draw a picture of yourself saying "Hello."

Hola from Spain!

Shalom from Israel!

DziÈndobry from Poland!

10

Bulletin Board Idea

Use the following bulletin board idea to introduce the section on foods. The patterns shown below make the bulletin board quick and easy to create. Begin by covering the background with butcher paper. Then use an opaque projector to enlarge and copy the pattern shown below. Finally, create the title "The Food Pyramid." As students make the recipes for this section, discuss where the ingredients fit into the food pyramid. You may also wish to place a table in front of the bulletin board to create a learning/research center to help students find out more about food and nutrition.

Food Pyramid

A Guide to Daily Food Choices

KEY

● Fat (naturally occurring and added)

▼ Sugars (added)

These symbols show that fat and added sugars come mostly from fats, oils, and sweets, but can be part of or added to foods from the food groups as well.

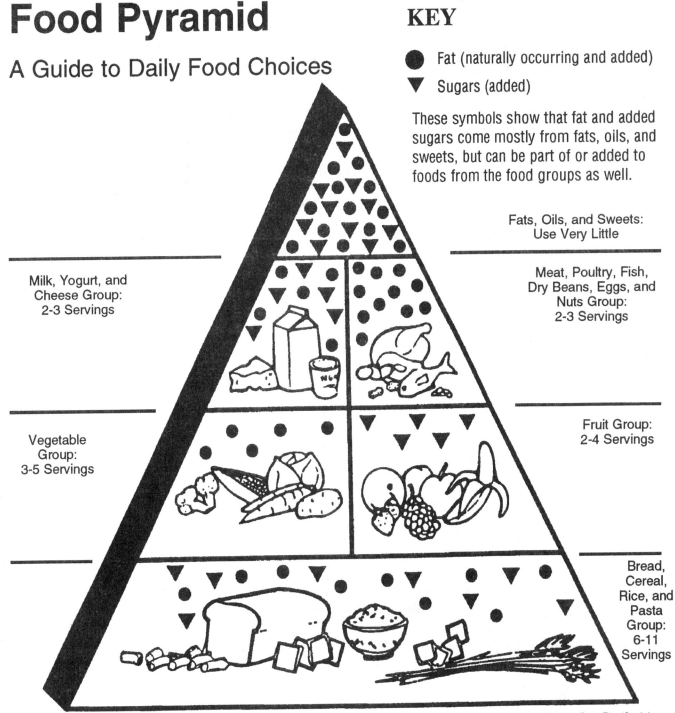

Fats, Oils, and Sweets:
Use Very Little

Milk, Yogurt, and
Cheese Group:
2-3 Servings

Meat, Poultry, Fish,
Dry Beans, Eggs, and
Nuts Group:
2-3 Servings

Vegetable
Group:
3-5 Servings

Fruit Group:
2-4 Servings

Bread,
Cereal,
Rice, and
Pasta
Group:
6-11
Servings

Introduction

One of the things that all people need is food. In this section, students will learn that some foods, such as bread, rice, and sweets, are eaten by everyone around the world. These common foods may be prepared in different ways, using a variety of recipes.

Sample Plans

Lesson 1

- Introduce the section on foods.
- Have students brainstorm a list of foods that they eat that come from different countries.
- Display the food pyramid bulletin board, and discuss the importance of nutrition (page 11).

Lesson 2

- Introduce the vocabulary for bread; then do a vocabulary activity (page 13).
- Select activities from Curriculum Connections (page 14).
- Identify common toppings put on bread (page 15).
- Locate the countries where some breads originated (pages 16 and 173).
- Bake breads that come from four countries (pages 17-18).

Lesson 3

- Introduce the vocabulary list for rice, then do a vocabulary activity (page 19).
- Select activities from Curriculum Connections (page 20).
- Read *Everybody Cooks Rice* (page 21).
- Choose activities for *Everybody Cooks Rice* (page 21).
- Create sentences about rice (page 22).
- Prepare rice recipes from four countries (pages 23-24).

Lesson 4

- Introduce the vocabulary list for eggs; then do a vocabulary activity (page 25).
- Select activities from Curriculum Connections (page 26).
- Use eggs for art projects (page 27).
- Write a story about being an egg (page 28).
- Prepare egg recipes from four countries (pages 29-30).

Lesson 5

- Introduce the vocabulary for sweet treats; then do a vocabulary activity (page 31).
- Select activities from Curriculum Connections (page 32).
- Make a word web about sweets (page 33).
- Name rhyming words for sweet treats (page 34).
- Prepare sweet treat recipes from six countries (pages 35-36).

Lesson 6

- Discuss the concept of meals and how it is a time when families and sometimes friends socialize.
- Identify the foods in a typical Mexican breakfast (page 37).
- Draw and label foods in a favorite breakfast (page 37).
- Identify foods in a typical Vietnamese lunch (page 38).
- Draw and label foods in a favorite lunch (page 38).
- Identify foods in a typical French dinner (page 39).
- Draw and label foods in a favorite dinner (page 39).
- Discuss where foods used in each meal belong on the food pyramid.

12

Background Information

Bread is the most commonly eaten food around the world. The first bread was eaten about 12,000 years ago in the area of northern Iran and Turkey. The people living in the mountains gathered seeds (grains) from cereal plants that were growing wild. They ground the seeds into flour, mixed it with water, kneaded it, and cooked the dough on stones that were heated by the sun. When these mountain people moved down to the plains, they learned that they could make more flour for bread by cultivating the seeds. It was not long before people from other parts of the Middle East as well as people living in Europe and India were growing seeds to grind into flour for bread.

One day people living in ancient Egypt found that they could make bread that was softer and lighter if they added yeast before the dough was cooked. The people living in ancient Rome also began adding yeast to their dough. They used millstones, which were heavy round stones, to grind the seeds. After the yeast bread had risen, breadmakers would knead it and bake it in clay ovens. The ancient Romans became quite skilled at making bread.

As time passed, many people wanted bread that was lighter and made from whiter flour. They discovered that silk sheets could be used to sift the flour and remove the pieces that were large and rough. Bread made from white flour was expensive and could be bought only by the wealthy. Most people continued to eat bread made from whole-grain flour because it was all they could afford.

Today people eat breads that are made from different cereal plants, such as wheat, barley, rye, buckwheat, millet, and sorghum. These breads come in all shapes and sizes. Some are leavened (made with yeast), and others are unleavened (made without yeast). Over the years, scientists discovered that whole-grain flour is more nutritious than white flour because it contains carbohydrates, fat, minerals, vitamin B, protein, and fiber that our bodies need. As a result, more people are eating whole-grain breads.

Vocabulary

You may wish to introduce the following vocabulary words at the beginning of this section: dough, yeast, all-purpose flour, self-rising flour, grind, sift, knead, bran, gluten, carbohydrates, fiber, leavened, unleavened, millstone, barley, wheat, oats, rye, buckwheat, millet, sorghum, bleached, bakery.

Vocabulary Activities

You can help your students learn and retain the above vocabulary by providing them with interesting vocabulary activities. Here are a few ideas to try.

- Have students work in small groups to define the vocabulary words and record the words and their definitions in a Class Vocabulary Notebook.

- Challenge your students to a Vocabulary Bee. This is similar to a spelling bee, but in addition to spelling each word correctly, the game participants must correctly define the words as well.

- Have students make a Parts of Speech Chart with headings such as Noun, Verb, Adjective, and Adverb. Under the appropriate heading, have them write each word in the context of a sentence, correctly showing its use as that part of speech.

Curriculum Connections

You may wish to use one or all of the following activities to supplement your own ideas about ways to integrate the *Celebrate Our Similarities* theme into your curriculum.

Language Arts:

Have students write a paragraph that tells the steps needed to make a peanut butter sandwich. After providing students with the ingredients for making the sandwich, have them trade directions with a partner. Then have them make a sandwich according to each other's directions.

Science:

Have students use a microscope to examine different types of grains.

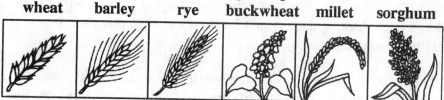

wheat   barley   rye   buckwheat   millet   sorghum

Social Studies:

1. Have students bring bread recipes from home and make a bread cookbook for the class.
2. Discuss how bread is made at a factory. You may wish to use the following diagram in your discussion.

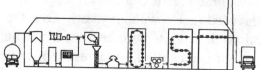

Math:

1. Have students practice using measuring tools (measuring cups, teaspoons, and tablespoons) that are used in the kitchen. Have them compare standard measurements and metric measurements.
2. Have students use a scale to weigh the same amounts of a variety of grains. Have them record their data on a bar graph.

Literature:

Read aloud books about bread. Have students draw pictures of the different types of bread that are eaten around the world. See the bibliography (page 174) for some suggested books.

Art:

Have students make different shapes, using cookie cutters and dough. The dough is made from 2 cups (500 mL) flour, 1 cup (250 mL) salt, and 1 cup (250 mL) water. Mix the ingredients in a bowl, knead the dough for about 8 minutes or until firm, and roll to 1/4 inch (0.6 cm) thickness. Have students cut out the shapes, using cookie cutters. Then place the shapes on a cookie sheet. Bake for 30 minutes at 325 F° (170° C).

Life Skills:

Invite a guest speaker from a bakery to tell how bread is made there or take a field trip to a bakery so students can observe the different steps in the process.

Bread Toppings

Many things taste great on bread! What do you like to put on your bread?

Directions: Write the word from the box that matches the topping shown on the bread in each picture. Then draw a picture of something you like to put on bread. Write the word for that topping below your picture.

Word Box
jam
tuna fish
butter
peanut butter
cheese

1. _____

2. _____

3. _____

4. _____

5. _____

6. _____

Breads from Around the World

There are many types of bread in the world. Here are just a few.

Directions: Work with a partner to label and locate the countries where these breads come from, using a world map. Then color and label the map on page 173 to show where these places are.

Tortillas from Mexico

Chappatis from India

White Bread from the United States

Irish Soda Bread from Ireland

Croissants from France

Black Bread from Russia

Flensjes (Pancakes) from Holland

Challah from Israel

Pita Bread from Greece

Pizza from Italy

Pretzels from Germany

Bread Recipes

Help your students make the recipes on this page and page 18 to give them tastes of breads from around the world. Explain to students that a recipe has ingredients, which are the things that go into making the recipe, and directions, which are step-by-step instructions for how to make it. Have students use the food pyramid bulletin board (page 11) to tell in which food group each ingredient belongs.

Have students wash their hands and collect everything they will need before beginning to make each recipe. Provide some kitchen safety rules for students to follow, and be sure they work under your supervision at all times.

Chappatis from India

Ingredients:
- 1 1/2 cups (375 mL) whole-wheat flour
- 1/2 teaspoon (2.5 mL) salt
- 2/3 cup (170 mL) warm water
- cooking oil

Directions:

In a large bowl, mix together the flour and the salt. Use a spoon to stir in the water, a little bit at a time. The dough should form a ball. Put flour on a cutting board. Knead the ball of dough until it is sticky but smooth. This will take about 5-10 minutes. Place in a covered bowl. Allow the dough to rise for 30 minutes. Cut or tear the dough into six pieces of equal size. Using a rolling pin, roll each piece of dough into a circle so it looks like a pancake that is about 8 inches (20 cm) across. Place some cooking oil on a paper towel and rub it on a frying pan. Heat the oil until it smokes. Place the dough in the frying pan and cook until both sides are brown and puffy. Eat immediately after cooking.

Maple Syrup Bread from Canada

Ingredients:
- 1 cup (250 mL) all-purpose flour
- 1 teaspoon (5 mL) baking powder
- 1 teaspoon (5 mL) baking soda
- 1/2 teaspoon (2.5 mL) salt
- 1 cup (250 mL) whole-wheat flour
- 1 egg
- 3/4 cup (188 mL) buttermilk
- 3/4 cup (188 mL) maple syrup

Directions:

Preheat oven at 325° F (170° C). In a large bowl, mix together the all-purpose flour, baking powder, baking soda, and salt. Stir in the whole-wheat flour. Beat the egg in a separate bowl. Then add the egg, buttermilk, and maple syrup to the dry mixture. Prepare a loaf pan by placing greased wax paper in it. Then pour the batter into the loaf pan. Bake for one hour. Allow the bread to cool and then slice and serve.

Bread Recipes *(cont.)*

Here are two more bread recipes that you can use with your students. Have students use the food pyramid bulletin board (page 11) to tell in which food group each ingredient belongs.

Irish Soda Bread

Ingredients:

- 1 ounce (30 g) butter
- 4 cups (1 L) all-purpose flour
- 1 teaspoon (5 mL) salt
- 1 teaspoon (5 mL) baking soda
- 1 1/2 cups (375 mL) buttermilk

Directions:

Preheat the oven at 400° F (200° C). In a large bowl, mix the flour and the butter. Stir in the salt and the baking soda. Pour in the buttermilk. Use a wooden spoon to stir in the buttermilk. The dough should be soft but not soggy. Rub flour on your hands and place flour on a cutting board. Place the dough on the floured cutting board. Use your hands to shape the dough into a round, flat cake that is a little more than 1 inch (2.5 cm) thick. Carefully sprinkle flour on a knife. Use the knife to cut a large X on the top of the dough. Use a paper towel to butter a cookie sheet. Place the dough on the sheet and bake for 40 minutes at 400° F (200° C). Serve the bread while it is hot. You may wish to put butter and jam on it.

French Bread from France

Ingredients:

- 1 package active dry yeast
- 5-6 cups (1.25-1.5 L) all-purpose flour
- 2 cups (500 mL) warm water
- 2 teaspoons (10 mL) sugar
- 1 teaspoon (5 mL) salt

Directions:

Pour the yeast into a large mixing bowl with the warm water and dissolve it. Mix in the salt, sugar, and 3 cups (750 mL) flour. Stir until the dough becomes smooth. Gradually add more flour, about 2-3 cups (500-750 mL), to the dough until it becomes stiff. Sprinkle flour on a cutting board and knead the dough. After about 10 minutes, the dough should become smooth and elastic. Place the dough in a bowl and cover with a towel. When the dough is double in size, punch it down and separate in half. Shape each half into a long loaf. Put the loaves on a cooking sheet and use a knife to cut slashes diagonally across the tops. Place a towel over the loaves and wait for the dough to double in size again. Sprinkle water on the loaves. Bake for 35-40 minutes at 375° F (190° C). As the loaves bake, sprinkle them with water to make the crust chewy. Allow the bread to cool slightly and then serve.

Background Information

Rice, like bread, is a basic food eaten around the world. Grains of rice come from a cereal plant. Long-grained rice and short-grained rice are the main types. Wild rice comes from a tall grass and is not considered to be "real" rice. Many people living in countries in the Far East, eat rice at every meal. These people usually eat brown rice. The rice is brown because it is still covered with bran. People living in the West usually eat white rice. The rice is white because the bran has been removed and the grains have been polished. Unfortunately, white rice is less nutritious than brown rice because of the bran removal process.

Rice is grown in countries such as China, India, South America, and Southeast Asia, where the climate is hot and there is a large amount of rainfall. Most of the rice grown in the United States comes from Arkansas, California, Louisiana, and Texas. Fields of rice are called rice paddies. The paddies need to be flooded. As a result, rice is usually grown near the coast or along rivers. In some parts of India and southern Asia, rice farmers depend on the water that comes during the yearly monsoon season.

Farmers prepare for each year's crop by plowing the paddies. Then the rice seeds are planted in soft mud called seed beds and covered with water. After the shoots sprout, they are transplanted into paddies that have been flooded. As the plants grow, the paddies are weeded and fertilized as needed. When the stalks are mature, they have clumps of grain that hang down. The husk, or protective outer covering, turns gold when the grains of rice are ready to be harvested. At harvest time, the stalks are cut, bundled, and dried in the sun. Then the grains of rice are threshed, or removed, from the straw. Farmers begin winnowing, which means they place the rice in a big shallow basket and repeatedly throw it into the air to dispose of any dirt or pieces of stalk. Finally the rice is taken to the mill.

Vocabulary

You may wish to introduce the following vocabulary words at the beginning of this section: cereal plant, polished, rice paddies, seed beds, shoots, husks, bran, stalks, monsoons, water buffalo, plow, threshing, winnowing, mill, long-grained rice, short-grained rice, combines.

Vocabulary Activities

You can help your students learn and retain the above vocabulary by providing them with interesting vocabulary activities. Here are a few ideas to try.

- On the chalkboard, list five vocabulary words to be Words of the Day. When students come into the classroom, have them use dictionaries to find the meanings of these words. Then have them share and discuss the meanings.
- Prepare a spinner to play Spin-A-Word by drawing lines to divide it into four equal parts. Mark each part with one of the following point values: 10 points, 20 points, 30 points, 40 points. Divide the class into two teams. Play the game by having each student spin the spinner and define a vocabulary word that you provide. A correct answer is worth the point value shown on the spinner. Then the spinner goes to the other team. A wrong answer means the spinner goes to the other team without any points being scored. The team with the highest total score at the end of a period of time that you designate is the winner.

Curriculum Connections

You may wish to use one or all of the following activities to supplement your own ideas about ways to integrate the *Celebrate Our Similarities* theme into your curriculum.

Language Arts:

1. Ask students to tell the class about their favorite rice recipes. Have them tell why they like that particular recipe the best.

2. Have students brainstorm a list of the different ways they have seen rice being prepared.

Science:

1. Have students do research to learn about the animals, such as water buffalo and camels, that are used in certain countries to harvest rice.

2. Show students a diagram for the parts of a rice plant.

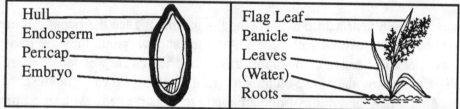

Social Studies:

1. Take students to the library. Have them do research to find out which countries in the world or states in the United States grow the most rice. Have them color a world map (page 173) to show where these countries are.

2. Tell students what monsoons are and how some rice farmers are dependent on rains that come during the monsoon season. Have students draw pictures of what they think it would be like to live in an area with monsoons.

Math:

1. Have students use a scale to weigh the same amounts of different types of rice. Have them record their data on a bar graph.

2. Have students plant some rice seeds. After the seeds begin to sprout, ask students to measure and record the growth of the seeds.

Art:

Have students make a mosaic, using different types of rice. Ask them to begin by drawing a picture on poster board. Then have them glue the pieces of rice down inside the different parts of the picture.

Life Skills:

1. Make arrangements for students to visit the cafeteria on a day when a rice dish is being prepared. Ask students to observe what the cafeteria workers do with the rice. After returning to the classroom, discuss students' observations.

2. Have students use chopsticks to eat rice. Demonstrate how one chopstick is placed between the thumb and forefinger. The third finger holds it in place. The second chopstick is placed between the tip of the thumb and forefinger. The middle finger is used to move this chopstick out and back.

Literature Connection

> **Title:** *Everybody Cooks Rice*
> **Author:** Norah Dooley
> **Publisher:** Carolrhoda Books (1991)

Summary: This is a richly illustrated book showing Carrie's tour through a multicultural neighborhood as she looks for her little brother. She sees people from different cultures cooking rice in a variety of ways. As Carrie wanders from house to house, she samples rice dishes that are prepared from recipes that come from Barbados, Puerto Rico, Vietnam, India, China, and Haiti. Carrie realizes that rice is a popular food in many places around the world.

Suggested Activities:

1. Have students predict what the book will be about by looking at the cover and the title.

2. Have students make collages, using pictures of rice and rice dishes from newspapers and magazines.

3. Discuss with students what kind of rice recipes are used in their homes. Have students bring rice recipes from home and create a classroom cookbook of rice recipes.

4. Provide a world map (page 173) and have students locate and color the places mentioned in the book.

5. Help students make the rice recipes shown in the book. Then have them sample the different recipes. Conduct a survey to see which recipes the students liked best. Then use the information from the survey to create a graph.

6. Have students write and illustrate new pages for the book in which Carrie learns about rice recipes from other countries.

7. Have students design a new cover for the book.

8. Have students make a big book that shows the events of the story. Ask them to share the big book with other classes.

9. Explain to students how to conduct an experiment with static electricity. Have them rub a balloon with a piece of wool. Then ask them to hold the balloon over the rice. The rice should be attracted to the balloon.

10. Have students role-play the story.

11. Provide different types of rice, such as quick-cooking rice, brown rice, long-grain white rice, and wild rice, for students to examine. Have students make a chart that compares and contrasts the different types of rice.

12. Have students work in cooperative learning groups to do research about the history of rice. Ask them to present their information to the class.

13. Ask students to write and illustrate poems about rice.

14. Have students use the calendar (page 157) and make a record of every time they eat rice. They should include rice eaten at home and at school on their calendars.

15. Ask students to make mosaics by gluing rice onto pieces of poster board.

16. Have students use the card catalog in your library to discover the titles of other books about rice available at your school.

17. Have students pretend to be grains of rice and write a class story to tell about their lives and what happens to them.

Writing About Rice

Directions: Write the sentence from the box at the top that tells about each picture.

Sentences

The farmers plant the rice by hand in the flooded paddies.
The rice is harvested using a combine, which is a large machine.
Rice is planted by airplanes that drop the seeds.
At harvest time, knives are used to cut the stalks of rice.
Water is sent through pipes to flood the fields.
Water buffalo are used to plow the rice paddies.

Growing Rice in Asia   **Growing Rice in America**

 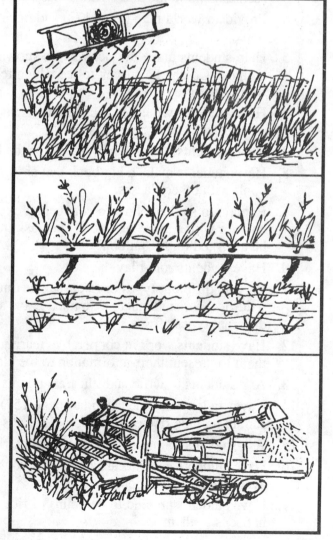

Rice Recipes

Help your students make the recipes on this page and page 24 to give them tastes of rice dishes from around the world. Explain to students that a recipe has ingredients, which are the things that go into making the recipe, and directions, which are step-by-step instructions for how to make it. Have students use the food pyramid bulletin board (page 11) to tell in which food group each ingredient belongs.

Have students wash their hands and collect everything they will need before beginning to make each recipe. Provide some kitchen safety rules for students to follow, and be sure they work under your

Spanish Rice

Ingredients:

- 3 cups (750 mL) cooked rice
- 1 can stewed tomatoes
- 1 teaspoon (5 mL) sugar
- 1 teaspoon (5 mL) salt

- 2 tablespoons (30 mL) butter
- 1 cup (250 mL) chopped green onions
- 1/2 cup (125 mL) chopped celery
- 1 medium green pepper, chopped

Directions:

Preheat the oven to 350° F (180° C). Begin by chopping the green onions, celery, and green pepper. Place the chopped vegetables into a large bowl. Use a large spoon to stir in the stewed tomatoes, sugar, salt, and butter. Mix thoroughly. Then stir in the cooked rice. Grease a baking pan and pour the entire mixture into it. Bake for 3-5 minutes at 350° F (180° C). Remove the rice from the oven and serve hot.

Jambalaya (Creole)

Ingredients:

- 1 cup (250 mL) cooked rice
- butter
- 1 pound (500 g) mushrooms
- 1 chicken, sliced into pieces (optional)
- 2 medium green peppers

- 2 medium onions
- 1 rib celery
- 2 pimientos, diced
- 1 1/4 cups (313 mL) canned tomatoes, drained
- 3/4 teaspoon (3.75 mL) salt

- cayenne
- 1/2 teaspoon (2.5 mL) paprika
- 1/4 cup (63 mL) melted butter

Directions:

Preheat the oven to 300° F (150° C). Put some butter in a frying pan and sauté the mushrooms. (Slices of chicken can be sautéed with the mushrooms, if desired.) Remove the seeds and membrane from the green peppers. Then chop the green peppers and place them into the pan with the mushrooms. Chop the onions and celery and add them to the ingredients already in the pan. Dice the pimientos and drain the can of tomatoes. Put the pimientos and tomatoes into the pan. Stir in the salt, a sprinkle of cayenne, and the paprika. Mix thoroughly. Then in a separate pan, melt 1/4 cup (63 mL) of butter. Pour the melted butter into the vegetable mixture and add the cooked rice. Grease a baking dish. Pour the rice and vegetable mixture from the pan into the baking dish and cover. Bake at 300° F (150° C) for 30-40 minutes. Serve hot.

Rice Recipes *(cont.)*

Here are two more rice recipes that you can use with your students. Have students use the food pyramid bulletin board (page 11) to tell in which food group each ingredient belongs.

Italian Rice

Ingredients:

- 1/4 cup (63 mL) clarified butter
- 2 cups (500 mL) rice
- 1 small onion, minced
- 8-10 cups (2-2.5 L) chicken or beef stock
- 1/2 teaspoon (2.5 mL) fennel seed
- salt and pepper, as desired
- 1/4 cup (63 mL) melted butter
- sautéed chicken livers and giblets
- 1 cup (250 mL) grated Parmesan cheese

Directions:

To make the clarified butter, place the butter in a pan over a low heat. After the butter has completely melted, allow it to stand and cool for several minutes. Skim the layer of fat from the top of the butter and pour the remaining liquid through a strainer into a large pan. Now reheat the clarified butter and brown the minced onion in it. Use a wooden spoon to stir in the rice until it has absorbed all of the butter. Add 1 cup (250 mL) of the chicken or beef stock and stir. Over the next 10 minutes stir in 2/3 of the stock. To the remaining part of the stock, add the fennel seed and stir it into the pan. Stir constantly until the rice has absorbed all of the stock. This should take about 5-8 minutes. Remove the pan from the stove and pour the rice into a large serving bowl. Add salt and pepper if desired. Stir the melted butter, chicken livers, and giblets into the bowl of rice. Sprinkle the Parmesan cheese over the top of the mixture. Serve immediately. (The mixture will become gummy if it is not served immediately.)

Bavarian Rice Dessert

Ingredients:

- 2 cups (500 mL) cooked rice
- 1/2 teaspoon (2.5 mL) salt
- sliced fruit (optional)
- 1 cup (250 mL) whipped cream
- 1 teaspoon (5 mL) vanilla
- mini-marshmallows (optional)

Directions:

Cook the rice and allow it to cool. Then in a large bowl, thoroughly mix the cooked rice with the salt, sugar, whipped cream, and vanilla. Add some sliced fruit or mini-marshmallows, if desired. Spoon the mixture into small paper cups and serve.

Background Information

In many countries throughout the world, people eat eggs that come from chickens. Mediterranean class hens, such as Leghorns, lay eggs that have white shells. Other types of hens lay eggs that have brown shells. However, the South American Araucana hens lay eggs that have blue shells.

White- and brown-shelled eggs are the most common and are equally nutritious. Eggs are a good source of nutrients, such as proteins, iron, phosphorous, and vitamins A, B, and D. However, they also contain cholesterol, a fatty substance that is believed to increase the risk of heart disease.

In the United States, eggs are classified and labeled as Grade AA, A, or B. These labels reflect the quality of the egg yolk, white, and shell, and the size of the air cell. Eggs that are sold for people to eat are not fertilized or have been stored in a cool temperature to prevent the development of the embryo. If the embryo has started to develop, the egg cannot be used as food for people.

Diagram of an Egg

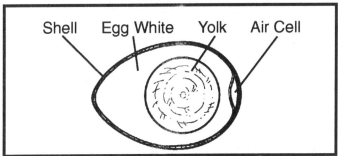

Shell   Egg White   Yolk   Air Cell

Vocabulary

You may wish to introduce the following vocabulary words at the beginning of this section: yolk, egg white, shell, air cell, fried eggs, poached eggs, hard-cooked eggs, soft-cooked eggs, coddled eggs, scrambled eggs, baked eggs, deviled or stuffed eggs, omelet, soufflé.

Vocabulary Activities

You can help your students learn and retain the above vocabulary by providing them with interesting vocabulary activities. Here are a few ideas to try.

- Using a newspaper, have students cut out the letters to form the vocabulary words. See how many words students can make in fifteen minutes. Have them glue the words onto butcher paper to make a class collage.
- Have students use the vocabulary words to create a word search or a crossword puzzle to exchange with a partner. Then have them check one another's papers.
- Have students create alphables by listing the words in alphabetical order and dividing them into syllables.
- Have students make a class recipe book that shows how to make fried eggs, poached eggs, hard-cooked eggs, soft-cooked eggs, coddled eggs, scrambled eggs, baked eggs, deviled or stuffed eggs, omelets, and soufflés.
- Crack an egg and show students the following parts: yolk, egg white, shell, and air cell. Then have students draw and label a diagram that shows those parts.

Curriculum Connections

You may wish to use one or all of the following activities to supplement your own ideas about ways to integrate the *Celebrate Our Similarities* theme into your curriculum.

Language Arts:

1. Ask students to brainstorm a list of egg-related expressions. Some examples include: "over easy," "sunny-side up," "walking on eggs," "smells like a rotten egg," "don't put all your eggs in one basket," and "don't count your chickens before they're hatched." Write their suggestions on the chalkboard. Discuss the meaning of each expression.

2. First, have students brainstorm a list of the ways they like to have eggs prepared. Examples include: scrambled, hard-boiled, and sunny-side up. Have students take a survey to see which way students prefer to have their eggs cooked. Help them show that information on a pictograph.

Science:

1. Have students test whether a hard-boiled egg will sink or float in fresh water and in salt water. Provide each pair of students with a hard-boiled egg, a jar filled with fresh water, and a jar filled with a mixture of 2 tsp. (10 ml) salt and 2 cups (500 ml) fresh water. Have students formulate a hypothesis, or guess, for what the egg will do in each type of water. Then have students test the egg in both types of water. Students should find that the egg sinks in the fresh water and floats in the salt water.

2. Have students determine whether an egg is cooked or raw by doing an experiment. Provide each pair of students with a raw egg and a hard-boiled egg. Have students spin the raw egg on a flat surface, momentarily stop it from spinning, and then let it go. Have students do the same with the hard-boiled egg. Students should notice that the raw egg continues to spin because its contents have continued to move even when the egg is stopped momentarily.

Social Studies:

Have students make confetti eggs for a holiday celebration. Have students prepare a raw egg by carefully poking a small hole in both the top and bottom of it while holding it over a bowl. Have them blow into one hole until the contents of the egg comes out of the other hole. Allow the eggs to dry. Then have students carefully enlarge one of the holes and fill the egg with confetti. After filling the egg, ask students to cut and glue a piece of tissue paper over the enlarged hole. During the holiday celebration, allow students to crack their confetti eggs.

Math:

Have students use a scale to compare the weight of an egg when it is raw to its weight when it is hard-boiled. Ask them to record their data on a bar graph.

Literature:

Read aloud a folk tale from another country. See the bibliography (pages 174-175) for suggestions. Then have students use hard-boiled eggs to create the characters in the folk tale.

After the eggs have been hard-boiled, use food coloring to dye them. Have each student cut strips of paper to use as collars for the character that will also help the eggs stand on end. Then have each student draw a character's face on the egg. Provide colored construction paper, yarn, and fabrics for students to use to add details such as hair, ears, hats, etc.

Art:

Have students color designs on hard-boiled eggs, using colored chalk that has been dipped in buttermilk.

Egg Art

Batik Eggs

Materials:

- eggs
- food coloring
- white crayons
- paper cups
- paper towels

Directions:

Step 1: Prepare the eggs ahead of time by cooking them until they are hard-boiled.

Step 2: Have students use a white crayon to carefully draw a design on an egg.

Step 3: Have students pour water into a cup until it is 3/4 full. Add food coloring to the water and mix thoroughly.

Step 4: Have each student place an egg into the cup until it is submerged.

Step 5: After each egg is colored, use a spoon to carefully lift it out of the cup.

Step 6: Allow the eggs to dry on paper towels.

Step 7: Display the eggs in a safe place.

Eggshell Mosaic

Materials:

- pencil
- poster board
- white glue
- yarn (any color or colors)
- scissors
- food coloring
- eggshells (cracked)
- waxpaper
- rolling pin
- paintbrush
- paper cups
- spoon

Directions:

Step 1: Have students use a pencil to draw a simple picture, such as a flower, on a piece of poster board.

Step 2: Have students glue pieces of yarn over the lines that they drew.

Step 3: Have students pour water into a cup until it is 3/4 full. Add food coloring to the water and mix thoroughly.

Step 4: Have students place their cracked eggshells in the cup.

Step 5: Carefully scoop out the eggshells for students. Place the shells on a paper towel to dry.

Step 6: After the eggshells have dried, have students use a rolling pin to crush them between two pieces of waxpaper. (If a rolling pin is not available, students can use a magazine that has been rolled up and taped.)

Step 7: Have students use paper towels to smear glue on an enclosed part of their pictures.

Step 8: Have students sprinkle the eggshells onto the glue.

Step 9: Ask students to repeat Steps 7 and 8 until their pictures are complete.

Step 10: Allow the pictures to dry. Remove any loose shell pieces by gently tipping the poster board.

Step 11: Prepare a mixture of glue and a little water. Have students "paint" this mixture over the shells on their pictures.

Step 12: Allow the pictures to dry thoroughly before displaying them.

An Egg Story

Directions: Pretend that you are an egg. Use the egg shape shown below to write a story about your life as an egg.

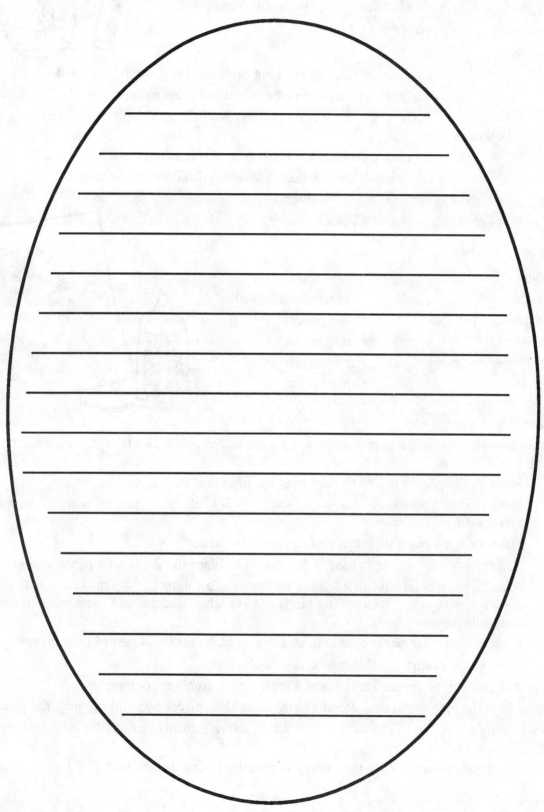

Egg Recipes

Help your students make the recipes on this page and page 30 to give them tastes of egg dishes from around the world. Explain to students that recipes have ingredients, which are the things that go into making the recipes, and directions, which are step-by-step instructions for how to make them. Have students use the food pyramid bulletin board (page 11) to tell in which food group each ingredient belongs.

Have students wash their hands and collect everything they will need before beginning to make each recipe. Provide some kitchen safety rules for students to follow and be sure they work under your

Mexican Scrambled Eggs

Ingredients:

- 4 eggs
- 2 green onions
- 1 teaspoon (5 mL) chili powder
- 1/4 cup (63 mL) catsup
- 2 tablespoons (30 mL) butter
- 6 ounces (150 g) tortilla chips

Directions:

Crack the eggs into a bowl and use a fork to beat them thoroughly. Stir in the chili powder and catsup. Then, over a low heat, melt the butter in a medium-sized frying pan. Thinly slice the onions. Place the tortilla chips in a plastic bag and crush them into small pieces. Place the onion slices and the broken tortilla chips into the pan with the melted butter. Cook slightly. Pour the egg mixture into the pan. Use a spatula to continuously scramble the eggs until they are cooked. Serve the scrambled eggs in small paper cups.

Frittata or Italian Omelet

Ingredients:

- 2 cups (500 mL) any combination of diced and cooked vegetables, chicken, ham, or seafood
- 6 eggs   • salt   • pepper   • 1 1/2 (23 mL) tablespoons olive oil

Directions:

Dice and cook the vegetables, chicken, ham, or seafood. While those ingredients are still warm, crack the eggs into a large bowl. Use a fork to beat the eggs until they are thoroughly blended. Pour the mixture of vegetables, chicken, ham, or seafood into the eggs. Use salt and pepper to season as desired. Prepare one 10-inch (25 cm) pan with a nonstick coating by greasing it with olive oil. In a second 10-inch (25 cm) pan, with a nonstick coating, heat the olive oil. Put the egg mixture into the pan of heated olive oil. Heat the frittata (egg mixture) until the bottom solidifies and the top looks creamy. Do not overcook it. Put the other pan upside down, like a lid, over the pan with the frittata. While holding the pans together, flip them over and allow the frittata to fall from one pan into the other. Then remove the empty pan from the top. Place the bottom pan back on the stove and cook the other side of the frittata. This should take about 1-2 minutes. Place the frittata on a hot platter and serve at once.

Egg Recipes *(cont.)*

Here are two more egg recipes that you can use with your students. Have students use the food pyramid bulletin board (page 11) to tell in which food group each ingredient belongs.

Egg Pancakes from Indonesia

Ingredients:

- 5 eggs
- 1 1/2 tablespoons (23 mL) all-purpose flour
- 1 teaspoon (5 mL) sugar
- 1 tablespoon (15 mL) soy sauce
- salt
- ground pepper
- butter, margarine, or vegetable oil

Directions:

Crack the eggs into a bowl. Then combine the sugar, flour, and soy sauce with the eggs. Add salt and pepper as desired, and beat the mixture thoroughly. After the mixture becomes a thin batter, strain it. Use butter, margarine, or vegetable oil to grease a small, nonstick pan. Then pour about 1 tablespoon (15 mL) of batter into the pan. Lift the pan. Swirl the batter around so it coats the bottom of the pan. Cook the pancake until the bottom of it has solidified. Use a spatula to carefully flip the pancake. Then cook the other side for just a brief amount of time. Do not overcook. Remove the pancake from the pan and place it on a plate. Grease the pan again and make the next pancake. Continue this procedure until all of the batter is gone. Use a knife to slice the pancakes into thin strips before serving them.

Chocolate Egg Soufflé from France

Ingredients:

- 4 eggs
- 2 tablespoons (30 mL) butter
- 2 tablespoons (30 mL) flour
- 3/4 cup (188 mL) milk
- 1/2 cup (125 mL) cocoa
- 1 1/2 cups (375 mL) sugar
- 2 tablespoons (30 mL) hot water
- 1 teaspoon (5 mL) vanilla

Directions:

Preheat the oven to 350° F (180° C). Melt the butter over low heat in a pan and stir in the flour. Pour in the milk and stir until the mixture thickens. Add the cocoa and sugar and mix thoroughly. Then stir in the hot water. Use two bowls to separate the egg whites from the yolks. Use a fork to beat the yolks. Gradually add the egg yolks to the chocolate mixture. Then add the vanilla and stir. Beat the egg whites until they are stiff and gradually combine them with the chocolate mixture. Lightly grease and flour a casserole dish. Pour the entire mixture into the casserole dish and bake. The soufflé is done when it puffs up and a straw stuck into it comes out clean.

Background Information

People have enjoyed sweets for thousands of years. Paintings found in caves show that early humans used to take wild honey from hives they found in hollow trees or caves. They did this regardless of the risk of being stung by swarms of angry bees.

Sugarcane was first grown on New Guinea, an island in the Pacific. For hundreds of years only the natives living on tropical islands in this area grew sugarcane. Then people in the Far East learned how to make sugar from the sugarcane. Traders from Arab countries took sugarcane to Egypt, Persia, and Spain. Then traders from Venice, who went to the Far East helped spread the use of sugarcane to northern Europe and England. Sugar became very popular. People believed this sweet substance had the ability to cure illnesses. As a result, sugar was used in many medicines sold in apothecaries (drug stores) at that time.

Many countries, such as Spain and Portugal, sent explorers to establish colonies in tropical areas of the world. Since sugarcane grew well in these places, huge plantations were started. The plantations grew, crushed, and boiled the sugar so it was ready to be sent for refinement in Europe. Today large sugar companies own these old plantations and supply two-thirds of the world's sugar.

Sugar beets are another type of plant that is used to produce sugar. For hundreds of years, people living in Europe used sugar beets in their medicines, as food for their livestock, and as a vegetable for themselves. However, making sugar from sugar beets was expensive and time consuming. It was not until modern machines were invented that sugar made from sugar beets could compete with sugar made from sugarcane.

In some places sugar comes from trees. In the northeastern part of the United States, many people enjoy maple sugar which comes from the sap of sugar maple trees. In the Eastern tropics and India, people use palm sugar which comes from the sap of palm trees.

Vocabulary

You may wish to introduce the following vocabulary words at the beginning of this section: dessert, candy, chocolate, confections, cookies, sherbet, ices, ice cream, mousse, parfait, pie, pastry, pudding, honey, jelly, jam, powdered sugar, brown sugar, granulated sugar, confectioners' sugar, sugarcane, sugar beet, molasses, maple sugar, palm sugar.

Vocabulary Activities

You can help your students learn and retain the above vocabulary by providing them with interesting vocabulary activities. Here are a few ideas to try.

- Have students work with partners to write riddles, using the vocabulary words as the answers to the riddles. Share riddles.
- Ask students to make a Sweet Treat Dictionary.
- Before students enter the classroom, hide index cards around the room, some with vocabulary words written on them and others with definitions on them. When the class arrives, divide them into two teams to play Vocabulary Hide and Seek. Allow students to search the room for a period of time that you designate. Teams can score a point by matching a word with its definition. The winning team is the one with the most points at the end of the time period.

Curriculum Connections

You may wish to use one or all of the following activities to supplement your own ideas about ways to integrate the *Celebrate Our Similarities* theme into your curriculum.

Language Arts:

1. Have students use rhyming words to write poems about sweet treats. Ask them to underline the words in their poems that rhyme. Allow time for students to share their poems with the class.
2. Ask students to pick partners. Then write the word chocolate on the chalkboard. Have students work with their partners to use the letters in chocolate to write as many other words as possible. Examples include: at, eat, coat, cat, to, too, hole, late, coal, hot, tale, let, cot.

Science:

1. Have students use a scale to weigh the same amounts of different types of sugar, such as granulated sugar, brown sugar, and confectioners' sugar. Have students use their data to make a charts or graphs.
2. Show students how to use a candy thermometer (to make recipes for sweet treats), for such sweet-treat recipes as candied apples or lollipops.

Social Studies:

1. Have students locate some of the countries in which sugarcane is grown. Ask them to color those countries on a world map (page 173).
2. Have students brainstorm a list of sweet treats that they enjoy. Then have them take a poll to see which sweet treat is the most popular.

Math:

Have students create simple word problems that involve sweet treats. Example: "If the class has already baked 24 cookies and then they bake 12 more, how many cookies will they have baked all together?"

Literature:

Take students to the school library. Have students work with partners to make lists of books that have titles that refer to sweet treats. Example: *Chocolate Cow* by Lilian Obligado.

Health:

1. Have students make a poster promoting the snacks that are sweet but still nutritious, such as fruits, juices, fruit shakes, and granola.
2. Provide cookbooks that include calorie charts for students to use. Have students work in cooperative learning groups to locate the number of calories in ten types of sweet treats. Ask each group to make a chart that shows these sweet treats in order from the least to the greatest number of calories per serving.

Art:

Have students bring candy wrappers from home. Ask them to glue the wrappers onto a large sheet of butcher paper to create a class collage.

Life Skills:

1. Invite a baker or candy maker to speak to your class about his or her profession. If possible have the guest give a cooking demonstration for students.

Sweet Treat Word Web

There are many types of sweet foods. Use the word web to name some of them.

Directions: Name four types of foods that are sweet. Then give four examples of that type of sweet food. One has been done for you.

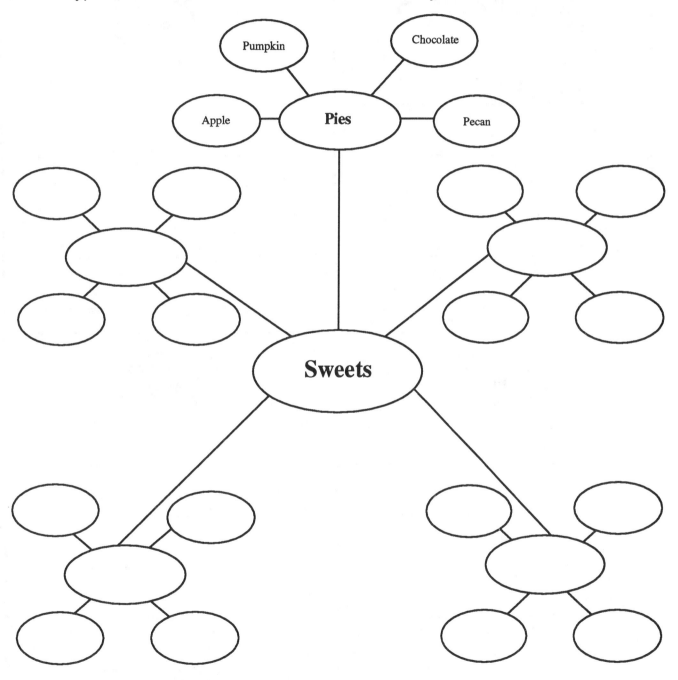

Sweet Treat Rhyming Words

Directions: Work with a partner to write rhyming words for the word at the top of each box. The first one has been done for you.

Sweet

1. treat _____
2. _____
3. _____
4. _____
5. _____

Cake

1. _____
2. _____
3. _____
4. _____
5. _____

Jam

1. _____
2. _____
3. _____
4. _____
5. _____

Pie

1. _____
2. _____
3. _____
4. _____
5. _____

What is your favorite type of sweet treat?_____

Sweet Treat Recipes

Make the recipes on this page and page 36 with your students, giving them a taste of sweet treats from around the world. Explain to students that recipes have ingredients and directions for how to make them. Have students use the food pyramid bulletin board (page 11) to tell to which food group each ingredient belongs.

Have students wash their hands and collect everything they will need before beginning to make each recipe. Provide some kitchen safety rules for students to follow and be sure they work under your supervision at all times.

Eple Kake, or Apple Cake, from Norway

Ingredients:

- 1 slice bread
- 1 tablespoon (15 mL) butter
- 1 tablespoon (15 mL) sugar
- 1 cup (250 mL) applesauce

Directions:

Crumble the bread and place it in a pan of melted butter. Brown the bread. Then add the sugar. In small bowl, alternate layers of crumbs and applesauce. Serve warm or cold.

Medenjaci, or Honey Sticks, from Yugoslavia

Ingredients:

- 1 cup (250 mL) margarine, melted
- 2 cups (500 mL) honey
- 2 cups (500 mL) all-purpose flour
- 3 eggs, whites and yolks
- 3 egg yolks
- 2 teaspoons (10 mL) baking powder
- 1 cup (250 mL) chopped nuts
- cinnamon
- powdered cloves

Directions:

In a large pan, heat the margarine and honey. Allow those ingredients to cool. Stir in the flour, whole eggs, egg yolks, baking powder, and chopped nuts. Add cinnamon and powdered cloves as desired. Place the dough on a floured board. Use a rolling pin to flatten the dough until it is about 1/2" (1.3 cm) thick. Use margarine to grease a cookie sheet. Place the dough on the cookie sheet and keep it in a warm place for about three hours. Then bake the dough for 30 minutes at 350° F (180° C). Remove the dough from the oven and allow it to cool. Then cut it into bars and serve.

Maple Syrup Tarts from Canada

Ingredients:

- 1 cup (250 mL) maple syrup
- 1 egg
- 1/2 cup (125 mL) chopped nuts
- tart shells, unbaked

Directions:

Crack the egg into a bowl and use a fork to beat it. Stir the syrup in with the egg. Place the tart shells on a cookie sheet. Pour the mixture into the tart shells and sprinkle nuts over the top. Bake the tarts at 400° F (200° C) for 20 minutes.

Sweet Treat Recipes *(cont.)*

Here are some more sweet treat recipes that you can use with your students.

Speculaas from the Netherlands

Ingredients:

- 1 cup (250 mL) sifted flour
- 1 tablespoon (15 mL) milk
- 1/2 teaspoon (2.5 mL) ground cloves
- salt
- baking powder
- 1 tablespoon (15 mL) candied fruit
- slivers of blanched almonds

- 1/3 cup (83 mL) dark brown sugar
- 1/2 teaspoon (2.5 mL) cinnamon
- 1/4 teaspoon (1.25 mL) nutmeg
- 1/4 teaspoon (1.25 mL) powdered ginger
- 1 tablespoon (15 mL) blanched almonds, chopped
- 5 tablespoons (75 mL) butter

Directions:

Preheat the oven to 300° F (150° C). Put the brown sugar in a bowl and add the milk. Stir until the brown sugar has dissolved. In a separate bowl, mix together the flour, cinnamon, cloves, nutmeg, ginger, a pinch of salt, and a pinch of baking powder. Cut up the butter and stir it into the flour mixture. Combine the flour and brown sugar mixtures to make a dough. Knead the dough. It should be soft and easy to work with but not sticky. Work the dough into a shape, such as a heart, so that it is about 3" (7.5 cm) thick. Add chopped almonds to the top of the dough to decorate. Use butter to grease a cookie tray. Place the dough on the tray and bake 30 minutes. Place it on a rack to cool.

Peach Melba from Australia

Ingredients:

- canned peach halves
- whipped cream or vanilla ice cream
- strawberry syrup

- pound cake, sliced
- walnuts or almonds, crushed
- cherries

Directions:

Put a slice of pound cake on a plate. Position one peach half on the cake with the cut side facing up. Use whipped cream or vanilla ice cream to fill the peach. On top of the whipped cream or ice cream, pour 1 teaspoon (5 mL) of strawberry syrup, add some crushed nuts, and crown with a cherry. Repeat the procedure to make additional servings.

Breakfast

Here is a picture of a breakfast that Mexican children like to eat. They use tortillas as their plates.

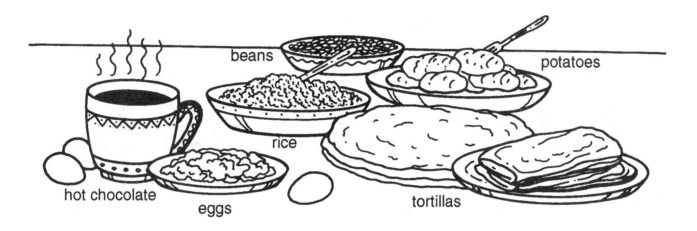

Directions: Draw a picture of your favorite foods to eat for breakfast. Label the foods in your picture.

Lunch

Here is a picture of a lunch that Vietnamese children like to eat. They eat their food with chopsticks instead of forks.

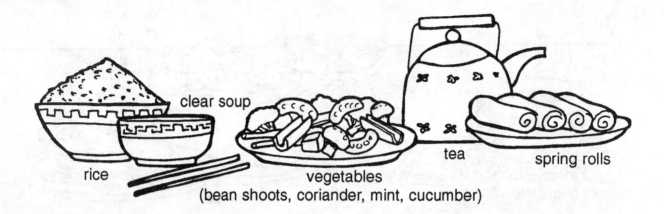

clear soup

rice

vegetables
(bean shoots, coriander, mint, cucumber)

tea

spring rolls

Directions: Draw a picture of your favorite foods to eat for lunch. Label the foods in your picture.

Dinner

Here is a picture of a dinner that French children like to eat. They use many herbs and spices to flavor their food.

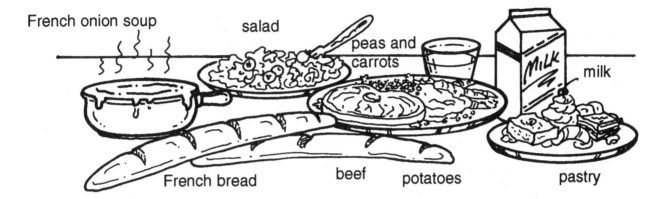

French onion soup   salad   peas and carrots   milk

French bread   beef   potatoes   pastry

Directions: Draw a picture of your favorite foods to eat for dinner. Label the foods in your picture.

Bulletin Board Idea

Use the following bulletin board idea to introduce the section on clothes. The patterns shown below make the bulletin board quick and easy to create. Begin by covering the background with fabric rather than paper. Use ribbon or lace to make the border. Then use an opaque projector to enlarge and copy the patterns shown below. Invite students to cut pictures of clothing from magazines and newspapers for each pattern piece. For example, they should cut pictures of different types of hats for the baseball cap pattern. Then have students make a collage by gluing their pictures on the appropriate pattern pieces. Finally, create the title "What Should I Wear Today?" You may also wish to place a table in front of the bulletin board to create a learning/research center to help students find out more about clothing. Use this table to display a variety of books as well as samples of different types of fabric.

Variation: Have students bring different pieces of clean clothing to display on the bulletin board. Use straight pins to hang up the clothing. Create the same title as suggested above.

Introduction

People from all over the world wear clothes. In this section, students will learn that clothing, no matter what the style or type of fabric, is still a basic need. People make fabrics for their clothing from available resources, using colors that are best suited for the climate in which they live. How the clothes are designed often depends on the environment and lifestyle of the people who wear them. For example, people who live in places like equatorial Africa, where the climate is hot and humid, usually do not wear much clothing. The perspiration on skin that is exposed to the air will quickly evaporate so the people feel cooler. However, people who live in places like the Middle East, where the climate is hot and dry, usually wear white woolen robes that cover their entire bodies. This type of clothing helps to protect them from the rays of the sun, the harshness of the desert wind, and the cold of the night.

Sample Plans

Lesson 1
- Introduce the section on clothes, using picture books of different countries or dolls dressed in the traditional clothing of different cultures.
- Display and describe articles of clothing from different countries.
- Make a clothing collage bulletin board (page 40).

Lesson 2
- Introduce the vocabulary for clothes; then do a vocabulary activity (page 42).
- Select activities from Curriculum Connections (page 43).
- Read *Hats, Hats, Hats* (page 44).
- Choose activities for *Hats, Hats, Hats* (page 44).
- Make a hat like the ones worn by Vietnamese farmers (page 45).
- Put together a Yugoslavian shepherd's hat (page 46).

Lesson 3
- Do a vocabulary activity (page 42).
- Select activities from Curriculum Connections (page 43).
- Create a collage of shoes from different types of pictures (page 47).
- Make a pair of Turkish slippers (page 48).

Lesson 4
- Make a Japanese kimono (page 50).
- Select activities from Curriculum Connections (page 43).
- Fashion some German lederhosen from some shorts (page 49).

Lesson 5
- Select activities from Curriculum Connections (page 43).
- Create a Spanish vest called a bolero (page 51).
- Make a type of shirt worn by Native Americans (page 52).

Lesson 6
- Select activities from Curriculum Connections (page 43).
- Put together a Chilean poncho (page 53).
- Draw a picture of some favorite clothes (page 54).

Background Information

Early humans, living about 25,000 to 30,000 years ago, probably made the first clothes to protect their skin from injury and to keep themselves warm. These clothes were made from animal skins and were pulled around the body like a towel. It was not until about 7000 B.C. or later that people began to grow crops, such as flax, and domesticate animals, such as sheep, for the purpose of making clothes. The yarn from the flax fibers and wool was placed on a loom and made into pieces of cloth. This cloth was draped over the body and tied at the waist. The ancient Egyptians, Greeks, and Romans wore garments fashioned in this way. By 1500 B.C. people living in the Far East discovered how to make fine fabrics using the thread of the silkworm. Sometime around 300 B.C. some Japanese found a way to weave a pattern directly into the cloth. Weaving became a special art during the Middle Ages. People frequently wore beautiful clothing made from velvet and brocade. Most European clothing continued to be produced at home until machines were invented during the Industrial Revolution.

The early colonists who settled in America had to be proficient in all tasks related to making clothes. They had to spin their own yarn, weave their own fabrics, and sew their own clothing. Shoemakers would either have a small workshop in the colony or go from door to door in order to repair or make shoes.

By the 19th century people wanted to be able to buy clothes that were ready to wear. Modern machines were developed that made this possible. Inventions such as the sewing machine allowed tailors and dressmakers to easily and cheaply make multiple copies of the same garment. As a result, store-bought clothes became very popular since most people could afford them.

Today people wear clothes made from natural fibers, such as cotton, flax, wool, and silk, as well as synthetic materials, such as rayon, nylon, and acetate. Huge factories are used to produce different types of cloth and clothing.

Vocabulary

You may wish to introduce the following vocabulary words at the beginning of this section: fabric, material, shoes, sandals, socks, pants, jeans, shorts, skirts, dresses, shirts, blouses, underwear, coats, jackets, hats, caps.

Vocabulary Activities

You can help your students learn and retain the above vocabulary by providing them with interesting vocabulary activities. Here are a few ideas to try.

- Have students work in small groups to define the vocabulary words and record the words and their definitions in a Class Vocabulary Notebook.

- Have students play Vocabulary Concentration. The goal of this game is to match vocabulary words with their definitions. Divide the class into groups of 2-5 students. Have students make two sets of cards the same size and color. On one set, have them write the vocabulary words. On the second set, have them write the definitions. All cards are mixed together and placed face down on a table. A player picks two cards. If the pair matches the word with its definition, the player keeps the cards and takes another turn. If the cards do not match, they are returned to their places face down on the table, and another player takes a turn. Players must concentrate to remember the locations of the words and their definitions. The game continues until all matches have been made.

- Have students create alphables by listing the words in alphabetical order and dividing them into syllables.

42

Curriculum Connections

You may wish to use one or all of the following activities to supplement your own ideas about ways to integrate the *Celebrate Our Similarities* theme into your curriculum.

Language Arts:

1. Have students say or write sentences about clothes that use possessive nouns. Examples: Nancy's dress is red. Peter's shirt has short sleeves.
2. Have students bring a variety of fabric samples. Ask them to touch each piece of fabric. Have them brainstorm a list of words that describe how the pieces of fabric feel. Examples: rough, smooth, silky, soft, bumpy, prickly, scratchy.

Science:

1. Have students bring a variety of fabric samples. Divide the class into cooperative learning groups. Provide a flashlight for each group. Have students direct the light from the flashlight onto each piece of fabric. Ask students to group the fabrics according to whether they reflect the light and stay cool or absorb the light and become hot. Ask students to tell what conclusions they can draw from this experiment.
2. Help students use plants to make their own dyes. Cherries, beetroot, and red cabbage can be used to make red dye. Onion skins can be used to make yellow dye. Spinach can be used to make green dye. Place a little water with the leaves or fruit in a pot. Bring the liquid to a boil, simmer for 15 minutes, then allow it to cool. Pour the liquid through a strainer or filter into a bowl. Then use a clean piece of white cloth to test the dye.

Social Studies:

1. Have students dress up in traditional costumes for a special holidays, such as Cinco de Mayo and St. Patrick's Day.
2. Take students to the school library. Have them do research to learn more about people who affected the clothing industry, such as Eli Whitney, Levi Strauss, and Isaac Merritt Singer.

Math:

1. Provide tape measures for students to use. Then have students work with partners and measure one another's height, waist, head, arm length, etc. Have students record their data on paper. Allow time for students to share this information with the class.
2. Have students determine what size shoes they wear. Then take a poll to find out how many students wear each shoe size. Have students record the data from the poll on a graph.

Literature:

Read aloud The *Emperor's New Clothes* by Hans Christian Andersen. Ask students to discuss and role-play the story.

Art:

Have students design some clothes that they think people living in the future might wear. Have them write paragraphs to describe the types of materials used to make the clothing.

Life Skills:

Invite a tailor or a dressmaker to speak to your class about his/her profession. If possible have your guest bring some of the tools used for making clothes.

Literature Connection

Title: *Hats, Hats, Hats*

Author: Ann Morris

Publisher: Lothrop, Lee & Shepard (1989)

Summary: This book contains photographs of different types of hats that are worn by people living in a variety of places. Some hats are worn for a specific purpose. For example, hats can be used for protection on some jobs, such as construction work, or for protection from the weather when it is rainy or cold. Other hats are worn as part of a traditional costume by members of a particular culture. Some people wear these traditional hats every day, while others wear them only for special celebrations. However, hats can also be worn just for fun. An index is included at the end of the book that gives an explanation about the hats that are shown.

Suggested Activities:

1. Have students predict what the book will be about by looking at the cover and the title.

2. Show the pictures in the book. Ask students to draw conclusions about what the environment or climate is like in the place where each hat is worn.

3. Provide additional pictures or examples of different types of hats. Ask students to describe the hats and tell what purposes they think those hats might serve.

4. Ask students to name different types of hats worn by family members and friends.

5. Have students brainstorm a list of careers that can be identified by the hats that the people wear. Examples: soldier, nurse, police officer, firefighter, construction worker, baseball player.

6. Provide a variety of materials, such as construction paper, fabric, and aluminum foil. Ask students to design hats for themselves. Then have students explain the purposes of the materials and designs they chose.

7. Ask students to look for pictures of people wearing hats in their social studies textbook. Have them keep track of how many hats they find.

8. Have students bring hats from home. Display them in the classroom by suspending them from the ceiling.

9. In your school or public library, locate books about magic tricks that use hats. Share some of these tricks with students.

10. Create a special celebration called "Hat Day." Invite students throughout the school to wear hats on that day.

11. Have students make a big book of hats. Provide one piece of tagboard for every two students. Ask each student to pick one type of hat. Have the partners draw and tell about their hats, one on each side of tagboard. Have two students design a cover and a back for the big book, using two pieces of poster board. Place the tagboard pages between the pieces of poster board and put the big book together using rings or yarn.

12. Take students to the library. Have them do research and give oral presentations about the types of hats that were used during different periods of history.

Vietnamese Hat

In Vietnam people often wear a non la. This hat keeps the sun out of their eyes while they work in the rice fields. In the central part of Vietnam, young women can pick a non la that has a love poem written on it. Use the following directions to help your students make a non la.

Materials:

- yellow tagboard
- red tempera paint
- paintbrushes
- red ribbon
- scissors
- stapler
- clear tape

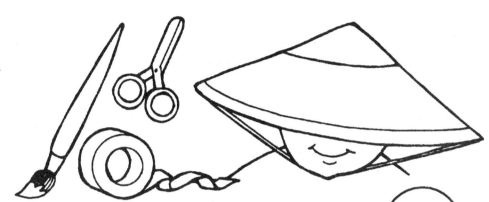

17 in (44 cm)

Directions:

Step 1: Help students cut a circle out of yellow tagboard that is about 17 inches (44 cm) in diameter. Mark a dot to show where the center of the circle is. You may wish to have the circles drawn on the tagboard prior to beginning this activity, or you can provide a poster board stencil for students to trace around.

Step 2: Have students use the paint to make a red circle that is filled in around the center of the hat.

Step 3: Then have students paint red around the outside edge of the hat.

Step 4: Allow the paint to dry.

Step 5: Show students how to cut two straight lines from the edge of the hat close to the middle. Be sure students do not cut the middle of the hat.

Step 6: At each cut line, have students overlap about 8.5 inches (22 cm) of the tagboard.

Step 7: Have students staple the overlapping tagboard together along the bottom.

Step 8: Help students tape along the open edge of the overlap to close the seams of the hat.

Step 9: Have students staple a piece of red ribbon to each side.

Step 10: Have students place their hats on their heads and tie the ribbons underneath their chins.

Ask students who else might use hats to protect themselves from the sun.

Everybody Wears Clothes!

Yugoslavian Shepherd's Hat

A shepherd is a person who takes care of a flock of sheep. In Yugoslavia, shepherds wear a special type of hat. Follow the directions shown below to make this kind of hat.

Materials:

- tagboard
- pencil
- ruler
- colored yarn

Directions:

Step 1: Cut a strip of felt or tagboard that is 3 1/2 inches (9 cm) wide and long enough to fit around the top of your head.

Step 2: Measure and make marks that are 1 inch (2.5 cm) away from one long side of the strip.

Step 3: Draw a line to connect the marks that you made.

Step 4: Color a design below the line that you drew. Above the line, cut fringe that is about 1 inch (2.5 cm) wide.

Step 5: Roll the strip into a band that is large enough to fit on your head. Staple it in place. Push down the fringe toward the middle of the hat.

Step 6: Place the band on a piece of tagboard and draw a circle around it.

Step 7: Cut out the circle and glue it onto the fringe to make the top of the hat.

Step 8: Cut about 20 pieces of yarn that are each 10 inches (25 cm) long. Hold the pieces of yarn together at one end and tie a knot to make a tassel.

Step 9: Glue or staple the tassel to the cap.

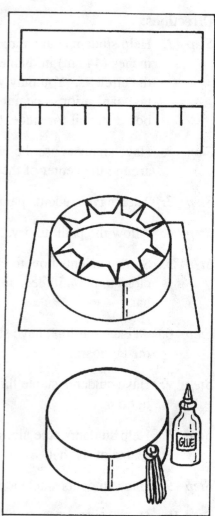

Shoe Collage

There are many different types of shoes. See how many you can find.

Directions: Use magazines and newspapers to cut out pictures of different kinds of shoes. Glue the pictures onto the footprints shown below.

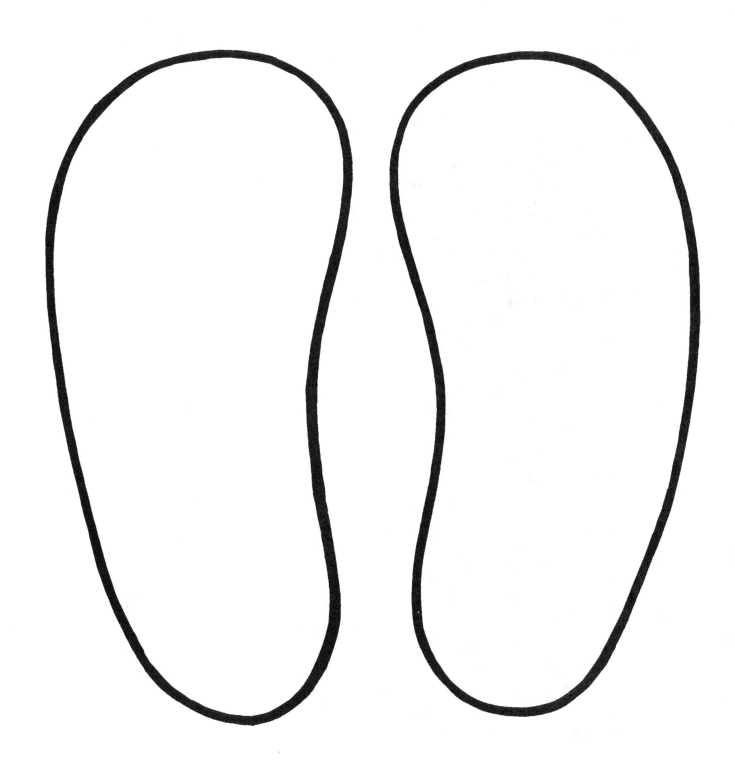

Turkish Slippers

Sometimes people who live in Turkey wear a type of shoe that is called a slipper. In this activity, you will make a pair of Turkish slippers. Have an adult show you how to carefully use a needle and thread before you begin.

Materials:

- pair of very large socks
- chalk
- needle
- thread
- scissors
- cotton balls
- two pompons or bells

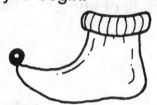

Directions:

Step 1: Make one slipper at a time. Put your hand in one sock and pull it inside out. Put the sock on your foot.

Step 2: Use the chalk to draw a mark where the end of your toes are.

Step 3: Take off the sock and place it flat on a table or desk.

Step 4: Carefully use a needle and thread to make a running stitch in a curved line from below your chalk mark to the toe of the sock. Be sure to make several stitches over the last stitch at the toe of the sock before you cut off your thread.

Step 5: Stick your hand inside the sock and pull it right side out. Make the toe of the sock come to a point.

Step 6: Sew a pompon or bell onto the pointed toe of the sock.

Step 7: Use cotton balls to stuff the toe of the sock until it feels firm.

Step 8: Put the sock on your foot and roll down the cuff. Now repeat the directions to make the other slipper.

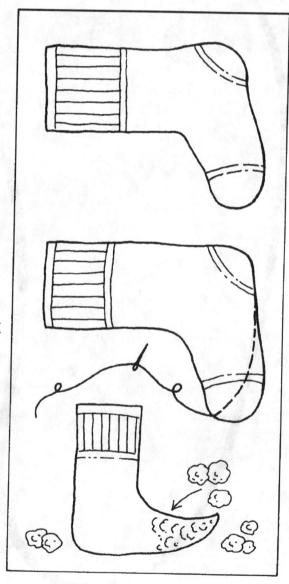

48

German Lederhosen

In Germany many people wear lederhosen, which are a type of shorts with suspenders. Work with a partner, and follow the directions shown below to make a pair of lederhosen.

Materials:

- tape measure
- butcher paper
- shorts that have cuffs at the bottom or that you can roll up to make cuffs
- safety pins
- glue
- scissors

Directions:

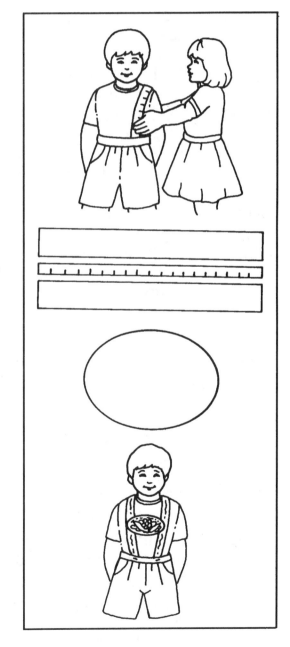

Step 1: Put on the shorts. Use a tape measure to see how long it is from the front of your waist over your shoulder to the back of your waist. Then add 2 inches (5 cm) to that measurement.

Example: 24 inches + 2 inches = 26 inches
(61 cm + 5 cm = 66 cm)

Step 2: Measure two strips of butcher paper that are 1 1/2 inches (4 cm) wide and the final length you got in Step 1.

Step 3: Cut out the oval shown. Then color the design. Glue the oval onto a piece of butcher paper and let it dry. Cut the butcher paper around the oval.

Step 4: Use the safety pins to connect the suspenders to the waistband of your shorts.

Step 5: Carefully staple the oval onto the suspenders so that it is over the middle of your chest.

Japanese Kimono

A kimono is a type of robe worn by some Japanese people. Work with a partner and follow the directions shown below to make a kimono.

Materials:

- a clean flat sheet
- ruler or tape measure
- rectangle of colorful material, 4 inches (10 cm) wide and 3-4 feet (91-122 cm) long
- straight pins
- chalk

Directions:

Step 1: Fold the sheet in half. Holding the two sides of the sheet together, cut a line that is 10 inches (25 cm) long in the middle of the fold. Then put the sheet over your head so it is inside out.

Step 2: Use straight pins to show where the sheet touches the floor. This will be the bottom of the kimono. Cut off the extra part of the sheet in the front and in the back.

Step 3: Turn up the bottom of the sheet and staple to make a hem.

Step 4: Hold your arms out straight. Use chalk to draw a line from each wrist to the bottom of the sheet. Be sure to mark the front and the back on each side.

Step 5: Cut along the chalk marks on each side.

Step 6: Hold the front and back of the sheet together on one side. Pull some of the sheet away from the body and staple a seam up to the waist. Do the same on the other side.

Step 7: Hold your arms out straight and staple a seam to make a loosely fitting sleeve on each side. Turn up the bottom of each sleeve and staple.

Step 8: Cut an opening down the front. Turn up the sheet on each side of this opening and staple.

Step 9: Take off the kimono and turn it right side out. Then put it back on. Wrap the piece of colorful material around your waist as a sash. Tie it in the back.

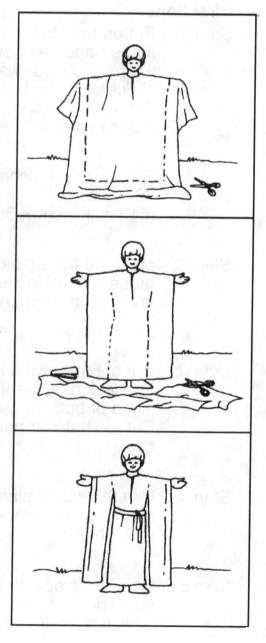

Spanish Bolero

Some people who live in Spain wear a vest called a bolero. Work with a partner, and follow the directions shown below to make a bolero.

Materials:

- butcher paper
- tape measure
- chalk
- scissors

Directions:

Step 1: Use a tape measure to see how long it is from your waist to the top of your shoulder. Add 1 inch (2.5 cm) to that measurement.

Example: 12 inches + 1 inch = 13 inches (30 cm + 2.5 cm = 32.5 cm)

Step 2: Loosely fit the tape measure around your chest.

Step 3: Cut a piece of butcher paper that is the length of your final measurement in Step 1 and the width of your measurement in Step 2.

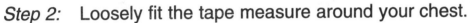

Step 4: Fold the butcher paper in half with the right side showing, and mark where the fold is with a piece of chalk.

Step 5: Unfold the butcher paper and lay it face down on a flat surface. You should still be able to see the mark you made with the chalk.

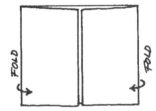

Step 6: Fold each side of the butcher paper over until the edges meet in the middle where the chalk mark is.

Step 7: Measure and mark 2 inches (5 cm) across from each corner at the top. Then measure and mark 8 inches (20 cm) down each side from the top.

Step 8: Use the marks you made in Step 7 to cut an arm hole on each side.

Step 9: Fold the butcher paper along the back so the arm holes are together. The opening for the front should be on your left and the fold along the back should be on your right.

Step 10: Use the chalk to draw a curved line along the front of the vest. Then, holding the two sides together, cut along the curved line.

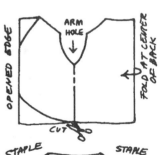

Step 11: Fold the vest again the way it was in Step 6, with the opening in the front. Staple along the top of each shoulder to make the seams.

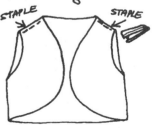

Step 12: Turn the vest right side out. Decorate it with crayons or colorful pieces of paper. Then wear your bolero.

Native American Shirt

Many Native Americans used to wear clothing that was made from animal skins. Each tribe had its own style of clothing. Follow the directions shown below to make one type of shirt that some Native Americans wore.

Materials:

- large long-sleeved T-shirt
- chalk
- felt
- glue
- measuring tape
- ruler

Directions:

Step 1: Lay the T-shirt with the sleeves stretched out on a desk or table.

Step 2: Use a tape measure to find how long the bottom side of each sleeve is.

Step 3: Cut two pieces of felt that are both 5 inches (12.5 cm) wide and the length that you measured in Step 2.

Step 4: Use a ruler and chalk to make marks that are 1 inch (2.5 cm) from one of the long sides on each strip of felt.

Step 5: Use the ruler and chalk to draw a line that connects the marks that you made in Step 4.

Step 6: Cut fringe that is about 1 inch (2.5 cm) wide along the bottom of each strip of felt.

Step 7: Glue one strip of fringe to the bottom of each sleeve. Allow the glue to dry.

Step 8: Use the tape measure to find the length around the bottom of the T-shirt, both front and back.

Step 9: Cut a piece of felt that is 5 inches (12.5 cm) wide and the length that you measured in Step 8.

Step 10: Repeat Steps 4, 5, and 6, using this strip of felt.

Step 11: Glue this fringe onto the bottom of the T-shirt. Allow the glue to dry.

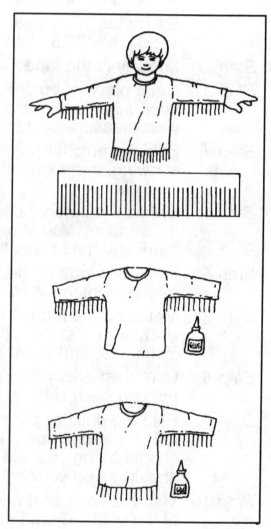

You may wish to paint or glue on some decorative bands. These bands hang over the shoulders, as shown here.

Chilean Poncho

In Chile, many people wear a poncho like you wear a coat. The poncho is made from brightly colored wool. In this activity, you will make your own poncho.

Materials:
- scissors
- glue
- red felt square that is 40 x 40 inches (102 x 102 cm)
- four strips of black felt that are 1 x 35 inches (2.5 x 89 cm)
- four strips of yellow felt that are 1 x 32 inches (2.5 x 81 cm)
- four strips of blue felt that are 1 x 28 inches (2.5 x 71 cm)

Directions:

Step 1: Cut the red felt into a square.

Step 2: Cut the strips of black, yellow, and blue felt.

Step 3: Place the red square on a table.

Step 4: Glue down the black felt strips to make a square inside of the red square.

4.

Step 5: Glue down the yellow felt strips to make a square inside of the red square.

5.
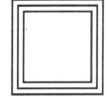

Step 6: Glue down the blue felt strips to make a square inside of the red square.

6.
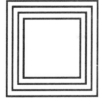

Step 7: Now cut a line that is 20 inches (51 cm) long in the middle of the red square.

Step 8: Put your head through the hole and wear your poncho.

7.
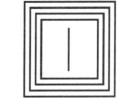

Your Favorite Clothes

Everyone has clothes that she/he likes best. Think about the clothes that are your favorites.

Directions: Draw a picture of yourself wearing your favorite clothes. Then write a short paragraph to tell why you like those clothes the best.

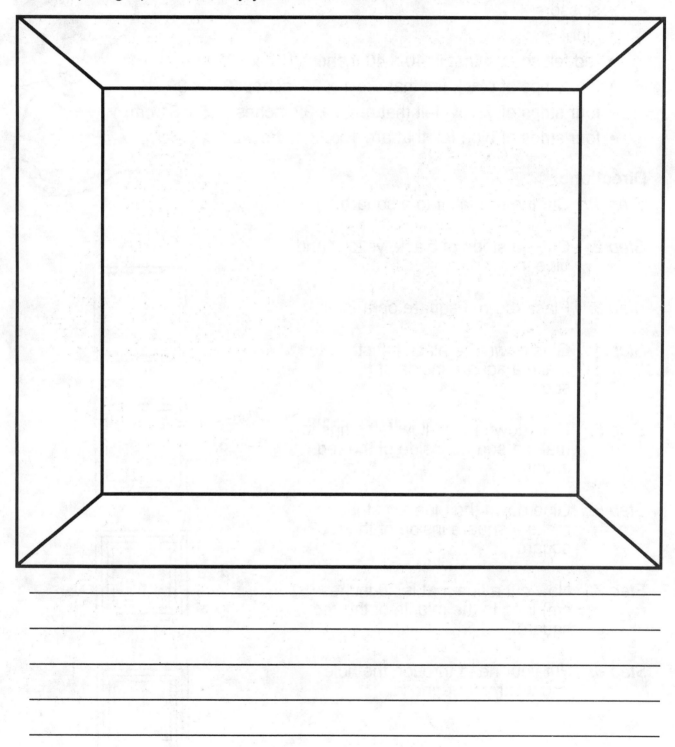

_____

_____

_____

_____

54

Bulletin Board Idea

Use the following bulletin board idea to introduce the section on the places where people live. The patterns shown below make the bulletin board quick and easy to create. Begin by covering the background with blue butcher paper. To create the appearance of curtains on a window, staple two long pieces of fabric at the top of the bulletin board, one on each side. About halfway down, pull each piece of material over to the side of the bulletin board and staple. Then use an opaque projector to enlarge and copy the patterns shown below. Finally, create the title "Home Sweet Home," and staple it in the middle of the bulletin board. You may also wish to place a table in front of the bulletin board to create a learning/research center to help students find out more about the places where people live.

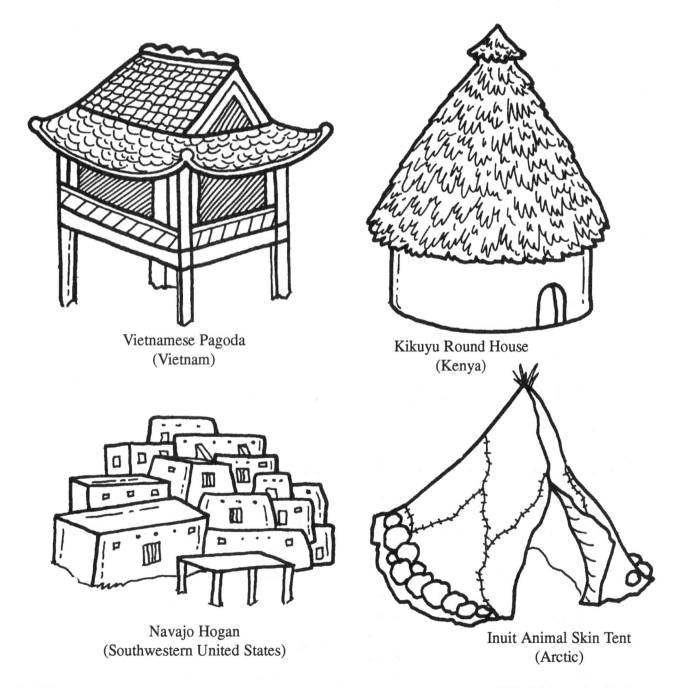

Vietnamese Pagoda
(Vietnam)

Kikuyu Round House
(Kenya)

Navajo Hogan
(Southwestern United States)

Inuit Animal Skin Tent
(Arctic)

Introduction

Shelter is a basic necessity of all humans. In this section, students will learn that people from around the world have a place that they call their home. One person's home can look very different from another person's home, but both places serve the same purpose by providing shelter. Homes are usually built using the resources that are readily available in an area. As a result, homes can be built out of many types of materials, including wood, clay, grass, bricks, and ice. Homes must be well suited to the environment and climate of an area, or they will not provide adequate shelter. For example, a grass hut would never provide protection from the cold and harsh conditions of the Arctic, and an igloo would never last in the heat of the tropics. Homes must also be built to accommodate people's lifestyles. In other words, people want to feel comfortable in the place where they live. Students will come to the conclusion that regardless of resources, environment, climate, or lifestyle, everybody needs a place to live.

Sample Plans

Lesson 1

- Tell about places that have been visited and describe the kinds of homes that have been seen in those places.
- Introduce the section on the places where people live.
- Display the bulletin board (page 55). Discuss the types of houses displayed on the bulletin board. Add pictures of other types of homes to the bulletin board.
- Describe and draw a picture of home. Tell why home is a special place.

Lesson 2

- Introduce the vocabulary for the places where people live, then do a vocabulary activity (page 57).
- Select activities from Curriculum Connections (page 58).
- Read *This Is My House* (page 59).
- Choose activities for *This Is My House* (page 59).

Lesson 3

- Do a vocabulary activity (page 57).
- Select activities from Curriculum Connections (page 58).
- Make a model of an igloo (page 60).
- Use a pattern to make a model of a tepee (page 61).
- Do research to find out what types of shelters other Native Americans used.
- Show pictures of apartment buildings.
- Create a model of an apartment building, using a variety of materials (page 62).

Lesson 4

- Select activities from Curriculum Connections (page 58).
- Do research to find facts about different types of homes.
- Make a pop-up book showing different types of homes (pages 63–64).
- Design a playhouse in the classroom (page 65).
- Vote on the playhouse design that is liked the best.
- Build the playhouse that was voted as the best.
- Draw a picture of the ideal house (page 66).

Background Information

Early humans took advantage of the environment and found places to live in caves or up in the branches of trees. These people did not need to build permanent shelters since they were nomads and moved from place to place in search of food. As time passed, some groups of people learned how to grow crops. Since these people stayed in one place to take care of their crops, they found the need to build places to live. Some built long houses consisting of several rooms. These houses were made from wood and clay and floated on a platform in a lake. Others built huts on the land. These huts were made from wood, stone, or clay. Usually a pit was dug under the hut so the inhabitants would have enough room to stand up.

Over time, different groups of people learned how to build bigger and better houses. People living in ancient Egypt discovered they could make homes out of sun-dried bricks, called mulguf. Ancient Greeks made sturdy homes out of stone, clay bricks, and wood. Romans living in ancient times built their homes of such materials as granite, marble, clay bricks, wood, stucco, and glass. By the Middle Ages, wealthy people used blocks of stone to build castles. However, most people lived in huts made from a mixture of wood and clay.

Today, people live in a wide variety of homes all around the world. These homes come in many different shapes and sizes and are built using a wide range of natural and synthetic materials. People continue to live in homes that suit a particular environment and climate. However, a person's lifestyle and feeling of comfort can also be important factors when choosing a place to live.

Vocabulary

You may wish to introduce the following vocabulary words at the beginning of this section: house, home, apartment, shelter, address, living room, dining room, bedroom, bathroom, kitchen, study, den, family room, utility room, garage.

Vocabulary Activities

You can help your students learn and retain the above vocabulary by providing them with interesting vocabulary activities. Here are a few ideas to try.

- Divide the class into cooperative learning groups. Then have students work together to create an Illustrated Dictionary for the vocabulary words.

- Challenge your students to a Vocabulary Bee. This is similar to a spelling bee, but in addition to spelling each word correctly, the game participants must correctly define the words as well.

- Have students make their own crossword puzzles or word search puzzles, using the vocabulary words.

- Divide the class into groups. Have each group be responsible for creating a game using the vocabulary words. Examples: Bingo, Wheel of Fortune, Jeopardy, Concentration, Spelling Bee. Have the class play the games the groups have created.

- Ask students to write stories, using the vocabulary words. Have them read their stories to the class. Then display their stories in the hallway for other students to enjoy.

Curriculum Connections

You may wish to use one or all of the following activities to supplement your own ideas about ways to integrate the *Celebrate Our Similarities* theme into your curriculum.

Language Arts:

1. Have students examine pictures of houses in magazines, catalogs, or newspapers. Ask them to pick one house and describe it. Tell students to be as descriptive as possible.

2. Have students tell about experiences they have had with moving into a new house or apartment. Ask them to describe how they felt about making the move.

Science:

1. Have students do research to learn about animal homes. Then ask them to tell how an animal's home in a certain region is similar to the homes used by people living in that area.

2. Have students describe how the environment or climate can affect the kinds of houses people build.

Social Studies:

1. Have students draw and label a diagram of where they live.

2. Ask students to draw maps that show how to get from the school to their houses. Then have them write sets of directions to go with their maps. Remind students they can use landmarks, such as a store or a large hill, to make their directions easier to follow.

Math:

Have students create simple word problems about building different types of houses. Example: If a couple of Inuit cut 31 blocks of ice to build an igloo and they had 7 blocks left over, how many blocks of ice did they use? (31 - 7 = 24)

Literature:

Read any copy of the traditional version of *The Three Little Pigs*. Discuss the different types of houses built by each of the pigs. Then read *The True Story of the Three Little Pigs* by Jon Scieszka. Ask students to use a Venn diagram to compare and contrast the traditional version and the retold version.

Art:

1. Have students staple together 20 or more small pieces of paper to make flip books. On each page, have students draw one picture that shows a different stage of a house being built. Students should be able to quickly flip through the pages of their books and see a moving picture that shows the house being built.

2. Have students paint a mural of houses from around the world.

Life Skills:

1. Have students work with family members to plan a fire escape route from every room in their homes. Ask students to describe their plans to the class.

2. Tell students to take out notebooks and pencils so that they can write down their observations of houses in the community. Ask them to pay special attention to how the houses are the same and how they are different. Then take students on a walk around the neighborhood that is closest to the school. Have them write down their observations. Upon returning, discuss what they saw.

3. Obtain copies of a change of address card from the post office. Help students fill out the card as if they have just moved.

Literature Connection

Title: *This Is My House*
Author: Arthur Dorros
Publisher: Scholastic (1992)

Summary: The text and illustrations in this book help students understand that people everywhere need a place to live. The book shows and describes a variety of homes lived in by children from around the world. The native language used by the children who live in each type of house is shown in colored print on the page.

Suggested Activities:

1. Have students suggest what the book will be about by looking at the cover and title.

2. Show the pictures in the book. Ask students to draw conclusions about what the environment or climate is like where each house is used.

3. Ask students to use small pieces of construction paper to make a mosaic of one of the houses shown in the book.

4. Have students make charts that have the following three categories: houses made mostly of wood, houses made mostly of stone, and houses made mostly of clay. Then have students write the types of houses shown in the book under the appropriate headings.

5. Have students pretend they want to buy some of the houses shown in the book. Ask them to write letters persuading the current owners to sell the houses to them.

6. Provide copies of the world map (page 173). Help students locate the countries that are mentioned in the book. Then have them color those countries on their maps.

7. Have students bring photographs of homes in which they have lived. Display the photographs on a bulletin board.

8. Have students write poems about the places people live. Allow time for students to share their poems with the class.

9. Have students make a time line that shows some types of shelters used by people during different periods of history.

10. Divide the class into cooperative learning groups. Ask students to brainstorm a list of ways to make someone who has just moved into their neighborhood feel welcome.

11. Write the word *apartment* on the chalkboard. Ask students to make as many words as possible using the letters from the word apartment. Examples: part, meant, meat, tar, pear, tear, rat, men, ten, rap, tent, map, nap, pan, pet, pen.

12. Have students brainstorm pairs of rhyming words with at least one of the words in each pair having something to do with the places people live. Examples: floor, door; wall, call; rug, bug.

13. Have a contest to see which student can use the greatest number of blocks to build a house.

14. Have students discuss the meanings of the following expressions:

    - That child is going to eat us out of house and home.
    - You better not say that because the walls have ears.
    - I went home to straighten up the house.
    - I just feel like hanging around the house today.
    - I will refuse to do what you say until the cows come home.

Igloo Model

Many Inuit, or Eskimo, lived in houses made of ice. They called these houses igloos. In this activity, you will make a model of an igloo.

Materials:

- cardboard
- white modeling clay
- pencil

Directions:

Step 1: Cut out a circle 5–6" (12.5–15 cm) and glue it to the cardboard. This will be the bottom of your igloo.

Step 2: Roll the clay into a ball.

Step 3: Form the shape of a cup without handles, using the clay. The sides of the cup should be about 1/2" (1.25 cm) thick.

Step 4: Make the opening at the top of the cup as large as the circle on the cardboard. You can check to see whether your cup is the right size by turning it upside down and placing it on the circle. Add more clay if you need to make your cup larger. Carefully tear away some clay if you need to make your cup smaller.

Step 5: After the cup is the right size, place it upside down over the circle. Gently smooth the bottom of the clay down onto the cardboard so it will stay in place.

Step 6: Flatten a small piece of clay into a rectangle that is about 1/2" (1.25 cm) thick.

Step 7: Slightly bend the rectangle to form the door of the igloo. Place the rectangle next to the upside-down cup. Carefully press the clay to join the two pieces together.

Step 8: Make the igloo look like blocks of ice by gently pressing the point of your pencil into the clay and drawing lines.

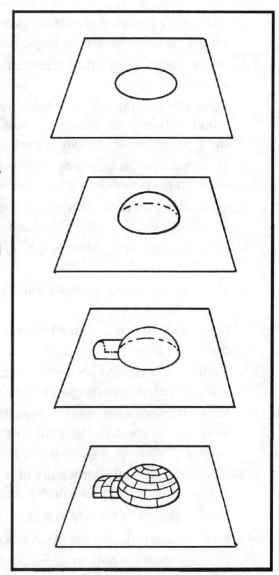

Tepee Model

Native Americans who lived on the plains moved from place to place in search of food. They built tepees made from buffalo skins and wooden poles. These homes were easy to set up and take down. Use the directions shown below to make a model of a tepee.

Materials:

- tepee pattern
- tagboard
- crayons or markers
- straws
- string or yarn

Directions:

Step 1: Color the tepee pattern on this page. Tepees were usually red, yellow, or blue. However, sometimes they were black, green, or brown. You may also wish to draw a design on your tepee.

Step 2: Cut out the tepee pattern, and glue it onto some tagboard. Allow the glue to dry.

Step 3: Cut out the pattern again, this time with the tagboard.

Step 4: Roll the pattern into an upside-down cone shape and tape it together. Do not tape over the door opening.

Step 5: Use the straws to make the poles for the tepee. Use yarn or string to loosely tie one end of the straws. Spread out the other end of the straws.

Step 6: Gently slip the tepee pattern over the straws.

Step 7: Fold down the two small flaps at the top of the tepee. These flaps were used to let out smoke from fires that were made inside the tepee for cooking and warmth.

Everybody Needs a Place to Live!

Apartment Building Model

Today many people live in apartments. Some apartments are new and modern buildings. Others are old buildings that have been changed into apartments. For example, some old castles in Europe are now used as apartments.

Look at the apartments shown on this page. Each one looks different, but they are all homes for many people.

Directions: Make a model of an apartment building. Use a variety of materials, such as boxes, clay, fabric, paint, and anything else you need to make your model.

Germany

The Netherlands

Canada

Southwestern United States

Book of Pop-up Houses

Materials:

- pop-up page pattern shown below
- scissors
- glue
- clip art (page 64)
- construction paper, tagboard, or poster board
- reference books

Directions:

Step 1: For each student, make six copies of the pop-up page pattern shown below.

Step 2: Have students cut out the pop-up pages.

Step 3: Show students how to fold the pages in half and cut the tabs.

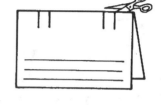

Step 4: Demonstrate how to open the pages and press the tabs so they stand up.

Step 5: Ask students to glue pictures of homes from page 64 onto each pop-up page. Allow the glue to dry.

Step 6: Have students glue the back of one page to the back of another page to assemble the book. Allow the glue to dry.

Step 7: Help students make covers for their books, using construction paper, tagboard, or poster board.

Step 8: Have students draw or color a background for each page. Then have them write one or two facts they learned about each type of home.

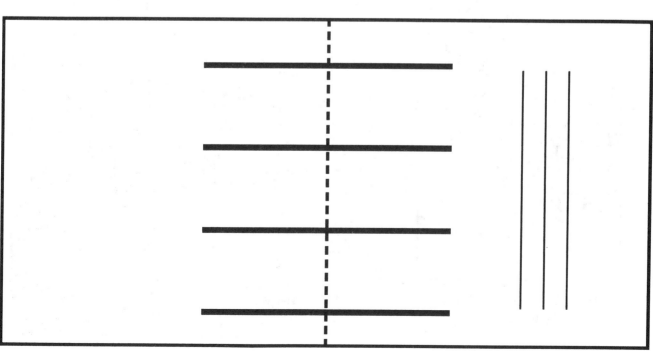

Everybody Needs a Place to Live!

Book of Pop-up Houses (cont.)

Directions: Do research to learn some facts about each of the homes shown on this page. Cut out the pictures of these homes. Glue one home on each page of the pop-up book you made on page 63. Then write one or two facts you learned about each home on the correct page in the pop-up book.

Arabian Tents
(Saudi Arabia)

Inuit Igloo
(Arctic)

Indian Pueblos
(Southwestern U.S.)

Iroquois Long House
(New York)

Chinese Junks
(China)

Swiss Chalet
(Switzerland)

Build a Playhouse

Think about what a house looks like. What is it like on the outside? What is it like on the inside? What type of things does it have inside of it? In this activity, you will work with three or four other students to make a playhouse.

Materials:
- a large cardboard box
- scissors
- tempera paint
- paintbrushes
- glue
- fabric
- smaller boxes

Directions:

Step 1:   Use the box shown below to draw a picture of what you want your house to look like.

Step 2:   Draw lines on your large cardboard box to show where you want your door and windows. Ask your teacher to cut these out for you.

Step 3:   Use a variety of materials to decorate the inside "walls" of your house. Use fabric to make curtains for your windows.

Step 4:   Paint the outside of your house. You can make the outside paint look like wood, bricks, stone, plaster, or anything else you like.

Step 5:   Use the smaller boxes to create furniture, such as tables and chairs.

Step 6:   After you have finished making your play house, invite a friend to come and visit!

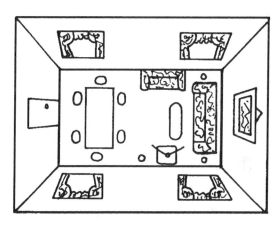

Your Dream House

Directions: In the box below, draw a picture of your dream house. This house should have everything you want or need. You can place your house anywhere you like. It might be in a tree, under water, or in space.

Bulletin Board Idea

Use the following bulletin board idea to introduce the section on communication. The pattern shown below makes the bulletin board quick and easy to create. Begin by covering the background with butcher paper. Then use an opaque projector to enlarge and copy the globe pattern shown below. Attach the picture of the globe to the bulletin board. Cut the letters needed to spell the following languages: GREEK, SWAHILI, ENGLISH, GERMAN, SWEDISH, EGYPTIAN, SPANISH, NORWEGIAN, ITALIAN, JAPANESE, ARABIC, FRENCH, HEBREW, RUSSIAN, CZECH, DUTCH, CHINESE, and FINNISH. You can add more languages, if desired. Then place the letters for the languages over the globe, as shown below. A variety of letter styles can be used to spell the different languages. Finally, create the title "Everybody Communicates!" You may also wish to place a table in front of the bulletin board to create a learning/research center to help students find out more about communication.

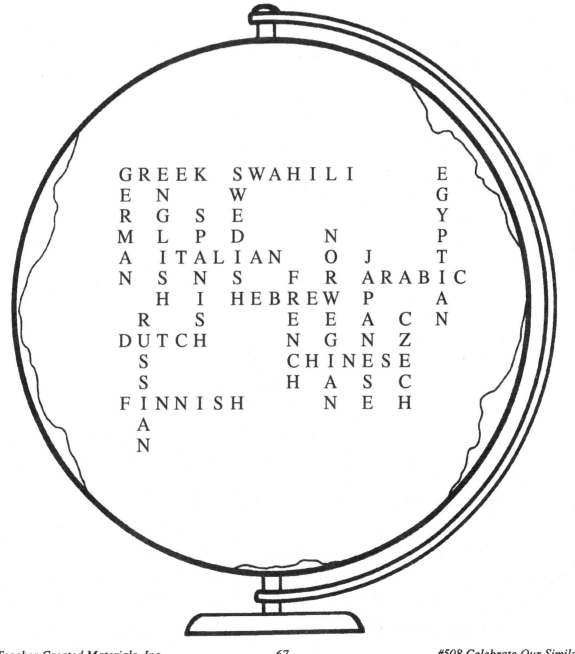

Introduction

People all over the world communicate with each other. Communication can be verbal or nonverbal. It can take the form of written or spoken language, pictures, signs, symbols, body movement, or facial expressions. Communication, in any form, allows people to share ideas and feelings.

Long ago, early humans first learned to communicate using grunts and gestures. Their communication was probably focused on their basic needs for food and shelter. Later these primitive people began to draw pictures in caves, on rocks, and in the dirt. As a result, they could communicate more complicated ideas, and they could share those ideas with anyone they chose.

As time passed, people learned to communicate in new and different ways. Society advanced technologically, and the volume of information increased at an incredible rate. People all over the world recognized the need for better and more efficient methods of communication. Inventions such as the telegraph, telephone, and computers have enhanced people's ability to communicate regardless of their locations.

In this section, students will learn that people all around the world communicate. They will recognize that no matter what form communication takes, it is an important way for people to share information and beliefs. But it also provides a way for people to tell about their hopes, dreams, frustrations, and disappointments.

Sample Plans

Lesson 1

- Introduce the section on communication.
- Brainstorm a list of ways to communicate.
- Display books that are written in different languages.
- Display the communication bulletin board (page 67).

Lesson 2

- Introduce the vocabulary for communication; then do a vocabulary activity (page 70).
- Select activities from Curriculum Connections (page 71).
- Learn how to count to ten in different languages (pages 72-73).
- Use foreign number words to answer questions (pages 72-73).

Lesson 3

- Do a vocabulary activity (page 70).
- Select activities from Curriculum Connections (page 71).
- Color flags according to a key that is in Spanish (page 74).
- Write Chinese characters (page 75).
- Use finger spelling to answer questions (page 76).

Lesson 4

- Select activities from Curriculum Connections (page 71).
- Learn the meaning of Native American picture writing (page 77).
- Play a matching game using international symbols (pages 78-79).

Background Information

The following chart shows a breakdown of the languages that are spoken from all around the world.

Language Family Number of Speakers	Indo-European (over 2 billion)	Sino-Tibetan (over 1 billion)	Black African (over 425 million)	Malaya-Polynesian (over 250 million)	Afro-Asian (over 200 million)
Languages Spoken	Albanian Armenian Bulgarian Czech Latvian Lithuanian Polish Russian Serbo-Croatian Slovenian Slovak Ukrainian Breton Irish Scots Welsh Dutch English German Danish Icelandic Norwegian Swedish Greek Bengali Farsi Hindi Pashto Urdu French Italian Portuguese Romanian Spanish	Chinese Thai Burmese Tibetan	Nilo-Saharan Languages Niger-Kordofanian Languages Khoisan Languages	Languages from: Madagascar New Zealand Hawaii Philippines Indonesia Islands in the Pacific Ocean Islands in the Indian Ocean	Arabic Hebrew Berber Languages Amharic
Language Family Number of Speakers	Dravidian (over 200 million)	Japanese/Korean (over 180 million)	Uralic/Altaic (over 125 million)	Mon-Khmer (over 75 million)	Others
Languages Spoken	Tamil Telugu Languages in: South India Sri Lanka	Japanese Korean	Finnish Hungarian Turkish Mongol Manchu Other Soviet Languages	Languages in: Southeast Asia India	Native American Languages Creole Pidgin English

Background Information *(cont.)*

Vocabulary

You may wish to introduce the following vocabulary words at the beginning of this section: communication, language, listening, speaking, reading, writing, foreign language, symbols, sign language, dialect, grammar, linguistics.

Vocabulary Activities

You can help your students learn and retain the above vocabulary by providing them with interesting vocabulary activities. Here are a few ideas to try.

- Ask students to write stories using the vocabulary words. Have students read their stories to the class. Then display the stories in the hallway for other students to enjoy.

- Prepare a spinner to play Spin-A-Word by drawing lines to divide it into four equal parts. Mark each part with one of the following point values: 10 points, 20 points, 30 points, 40 points. Divide the class into two teams. Play the game by having each student spin the spinner and define a vocabulary word that you provide. A correct answer is worth the point value shown on the spinner. Then the spinner goes to the other team. A wrong answer means the spinner goes to the other team without any points being scored. The team with the highest total score at the end of a period of time that you designate is the winner.

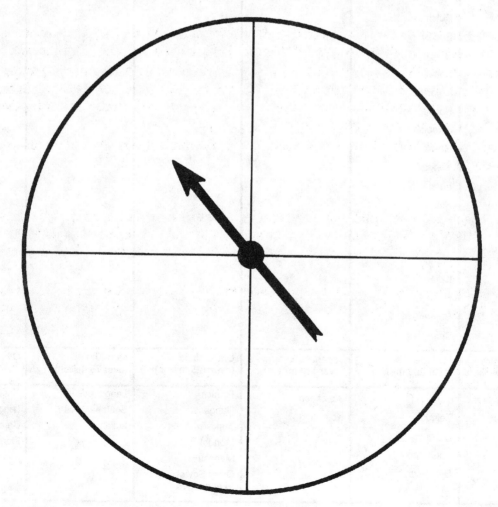

70

Curriculum Connections

You may wish to use one or all of the following activities to supplement your own ideas about ways to integrate the *Celebrate Our Similarities* theme into your curriculum.

Language Arts:

1. Conduct an activity in which students have to use nonverbal communication to do something cooperatively. Stress to students that they are not allowed to talk at all during the activity.

2. Have students invent their own symbols for each letter of the alphabet. Then have them write messages using these symbols. Ask students to trade papers with partners and decode each other's messages.

3. Provide examples or have students brainstorm a list of English words that have been borrowed from foreign languages. Examples: pasta (Italy), banjo (African), piano (Italian), chef (French), igloo (Eskimo), karate (Japanese), tepee (Native American), tea (Chinese), kindergarten (German), exit (Latin), pajamas (Hindi).

Science:

1. Have students research an invention, such as the telegraph or telephone, that helped improve people's ability to communicate with each other over long distances.

2. Have pairs of students work together to make a telephone, using two clean paper cups and some string. Take students outside where they use their telephones to communicate.

Social Studies:

1. Have students listen to folk songs from other countries. Then ask them to describe what the songs are about. See the bibliography (page 174) for a list of suggested folk music.

2. Provide copies of the world map (page 173). Have students work together in groups to identify countries that speak the same language. For example, most of the people living in the United States, Canada, Great Britain, and Australia speak English. Ask students to color the map to show the countries where a particular language is spoken.

3. Invite an older student who is a Boy Scout to teach your class how to spell words using the Semaphore Code.

Math:

1. Have students use paper plates to make clocks. The clock hands can be made from poster board and attached to the plates with brads. Ask students to write Chinese numerals (page 75) on the faces of their clocks. You may wish to have students make additional clocks with numerals from other languages, too.

2. Have students read books about how to count numbers using the languages spoken in such places as the Arab countries, China, Japan, and Mexico. See bibliography (page 174) for suggestions.

Literature:

Display books that are written in a variety of foreign languages. Allow students time to look at the books. Have them discuss what they think the books are about. Ask them to tell what clues gave them information about the contents of the books.

Art:

Have students paint or draw pictures of how they would communicate with a creature who was visiting from another planet.

Everybody Communicates!

Numbers from Around the World

Directions: Look at the chart. Read the number words that are written in English, French, Greek, German, and Spanish. Then write the correct number words in the blanks at the bottom of the page.

ENGLISH	FRENCH	GREEK	GERMAN	SPANISH
one	un	ena	eins	uno
two	deux	dyo	zwei	dos
three	trois	tria	drei	tres
four	quatre	tessara	vier	quatro
five	cinq	pente	funf	cinco
six	six	exi	sechs	seis
seven	sept	epta	sieben	siete
eight	huit	okto	acht	ocho
nine	neuf	ennea	neun	nueve
ten	dix	deka	zehn	diez

1. Write the French word that tells how old you are. _____

2. Write the Greek word that tells how many vases you see. _____

3. Write the Spanish word that tells how many piñatas you see. _____

4. Write the German word that tells how many castles you see. _____

5. Write the French word that tells how many loaves of bread you see. _____

6. Write the Spanish word that tells how many sombreros you see. _____

7. Write the German word that tells how many gingerbread people you see. _____

8. Write the Greek word that tells how many olives you see. _____

Numbers from Around the World *(cont.)*

Directions: Look at the chart. Read the number words that are written in English, Indian, Mandarin, Tagalog, and Japanese. Then write the correct number words in the blanks at the bottom of the page.

ENGLISH	INDIAN (India)	MANDARIN (China)	TAGALOG (Philippines)	JAPANESE
one	Ek	yī	isa	ichi
two	Do	èr	dalawa	ni
three	Teen	sān	tatlo	san
four	Chár	sì	apat	shi
five	Panch	wū	lima	go
six	Chey	liù	anim	roku
seven	Saat	qī	pito	shichi
eight	Āth	bā	walo	hachi
nine	Nau	jiū	siyam	ku
ten	Dus	shí	sampû	ju

1. Write the Mandarin word that tells how many water buffalo you see.

   _____

2. Write the Japanese word that tells how many pairs of chopsticks you see.

   _____

3. Write the Tagalog word that tells how many bowls of rice you see.

   _____

4. Write the Indian word that tells how many turbans you see.

   _____

5. Write the Japanese word that tells how many fans you see.

   _____

6. Write the Indian word that tells how many tigers you see.

   _____

7. Write the Mandarin word that tells how many lanterns you see.

   _____

8. Write the Tagalog word that tells how many coconuts you see.

   _____

Spanish Color Words

Directions: Use the words that are written in Spanish to color the flags. Most of the people in these countries speak Spanish.

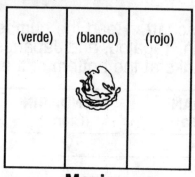

Mexico

Word Box

amarillo = yellow

azul = blue

blanco = white

rojo = red

verde = green

(rojo)

(amarillo)

(verde)

Bolivia

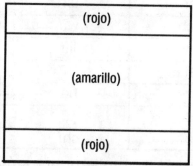

Spain

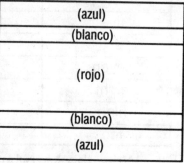

Costa Rica

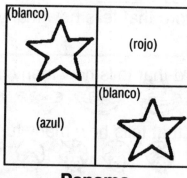

Panama

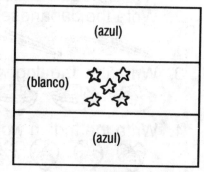

Honduras

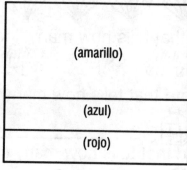

Columbia

(rojo)

(blanco)

(azul)

Paraguay

Writing in Chinese

The Chinese began using a written language about 3500 years ago. This written language has characters rather than an alphabet. There are thousands of characters. Each one stands for a different word.

Directions: Use a black marker, a black crayon, or a small paintbrush and black paint to write the characters shown below.

English	Chinese	Your Turn
one	一	
two	二	
three	三	
four	四	
five	五	
six	六	
seven	七	
eight	八	
nine	九	
ten	十	

English	Chinese	Your Turn
child	子	
woman	女	
man	人	
sun	☉	
moon	月	
river	川	
fire	火	
wood	木	
rice	米	
good luck	吉	

Using Your Hands to Talk

Some people cannot hear very well. Others cannot hear at all. Some of these people use their hands to talk. Work with a partner and learn how to talk by spelling words with your hands.

Finger Spelling

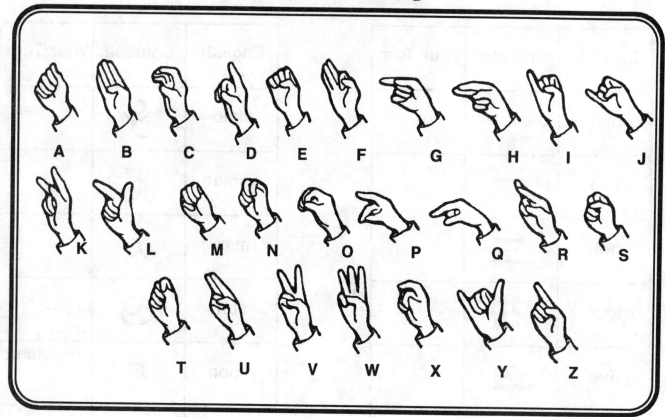

Directions: Use your hands to tell your partner the answers to these questions.

1. What is your name?

2. What is your favorite color?

3. What is your favorite food?

4. What is the name of the street where you live?

5. In which month were you born?

Native American Picture Writing

Long ago Native Americans used a type of writing that was done in the form of pictures. The pictures were drawn in the dirt or painted on rocks and in caves. Some of these pictures are shown below.

sun	rain	tepee	buffalo
moon	man	food	hello
water	woman	bird	baby

Directions: Study the pictures and what they mean. Make up some of your own symbols by drawing pictures and telling what they mean. Then use pictures to write a note. Ask a friend to decode your note.

My Picture Symbols

My Note

International Symbols Game

Some symbols are used all over the world so everyone will know what they mean. A few of these symbols are shown below.

Directions: Work with a partner. Study the symbols on this page. Learn the meanings of these symbols, using page 79. Then cut out the cards on both pages. Mix up the cards and lay them face down. Take turns trying to match each symbol with its meaning. The person with the most pairs wins.

International Symbols
Game *(cont.)*

Directions: Use these cards to learn the meanings of the symbols shown on page 78. Then use the rules on page 78 to play the game.

STOP	FIRST AID	TELEPHONE	RESTAURANT
NO LEFT TURN	MEN'S BATHROOM	WOMEN'S BATHROOM	INFORMATION
NO BICYCLES	DO NOT ENTER	HOSPITAL	GAS STATION
ICE HOCKEY RINK	SWIMMING AREA	HORSEBACK RIDING AREA	BASKETBALL COURT
BUS STATION	AIRPORT	POISONOUS	NO SMOKING

Bulletin Board Idea

Use the following bulletin board idea to introduce the section on transportation. The patterns shown below make the bulletin board quick and easy to create. Begin by creating a background that looks like an outdoor scene. First cover the entire bulletin board with blue butcher paper. Then cut some green butcher paper or use green indoor/outdoor carpeting to make some rolling hills along the bottom of the bulletin board. Create a lake with blue paper. Then use white cotton balls to make some clouds in the sky. Next use an opaque projector to enlarge and copy the patterns shown below. Finally, create the title "Transportation." You may also wish to place a table in front of the bulletin board to create a learning/research center to help students find out more about transportation.

Introduction

In this section, students will learn that people all around the world use transportation to travel from place to place. People can travel to places that are close to where they live, such as schools and grocery stores. But they can also travel to places that are far away, such as other cities, states, and countries. Today, there are many different types of land, water, and air transportation available. Sometimes people need to travel on land. To do this, they can use animals such as camels, horses, burros, and elephants; human-powered vehicles such as bicycles or rickshas; or mechanically run vehicles such as cars, trucks, buses, trains, and monorails. At other times, people need to travel on or in the water. Ways to travel by water include sailboats, motorboats, ships, canoes, ferries, barges, hovercrafts, and submarines. Another way people might travel is by air. Planes, jets, helicopters, gliders, and hot air balloons are some of the vehicles used to travel by air. Regardless of the type of transportation people use, they always find a way to travel from place to place. For this reason, students will realize that using transportation is one of the ways in which people from all around the world are similar.

Sample Plans

Lesson 1

- Introduce the section on transportation.
- Brainstorm a list of ways to travel.
- Show books about different types of transportation.
- Display model boats, cars, trains, planes, etc.
- Create the transportation bulletin board (page 80).

Lesson 2

- Introduce the vocabulary for transportation; then do a vocabulary activity (page 82).
- Select activities from Curriculum Connections (page 83).
- Discuss how people in the local community travel from place to place.
- Determine whether different types of transportation are used for land, water, or air travel (page 84).
- Make a model of a car that moves by using a magnet (page 85).

Lesson 3

- Do a vocabulary activity (page 82).
- Select activities from Curriculum Connections (page 83).
- Make a model of a canoe (page 86).
- Create and fly a model of a hot air balloon (page 87).

Lesson 4

- Select activities from Curriculum Connections (page 83).
- Race a model boat (page 88).
- Invent a method of transportation that will be used by people living in the future (page 89).

Background Information

The following time line shows some of the important developments in the area of transportation.

Transportation Time Line:

5000-3500 B.C.	Donkeys and oxen were used as beasts of burden.
3500-3200 B.C.	The wheel was invented by people in Mesopotamia.
	Sails were invented by the Egyptians.
300 B.C.-A.D. 300	A system of paved roads was built by the Romans.
800-1200	Europeans invented a harness for horses.
	Wagons were built.
1400-1500	Coaches with spring suspension systems were used.
	Sailing ships improved so that people could travel across the ocean.
1700-1800	The steam engine was invented in Great Britain.
1800-1900	People in Great Britain started using steam powered trains.
	Gasoline engines were invented and used to power bicycles in Germany.
	Gasoline engines were used inside the frame of an automobile in France.
1900-1920	The Wright brothers successfully flew an airplane.
1920-1930	Cars became a popular means of transportation in the United States.
1950-1960	Jet airplanes were used for commercial flights.
1970-1980	The Concorde, which is capable of supersonic flight, was used for traveling between Europe and the United States.

Vocabulary

You may wish to introduce the following vocabulary words at the beginning of this section: transportation, train, subway, monorail, car, truck, airplane, jet, sled, boat, ship, space shuttle, barge, raft, blimp, hot air balloon, bus, kayak, steamship, glider, bicycle, moped, motorcycle, snowmobile, submarine, helicopter, hovercraft, canoe, cart, wagon, ricksha, camel, horse, elephant, mule, donkey.

Vocabulary Activities

You can help your students learn and retain the above vocabulary by providing them with interesting vocabulary activities. Here are a few ideas to try.

* Have students play Vocabulary Charades by acting out the vocabulary words.
* Divide the class into cooperative learning groups. Then have students work together to create an Illustrated Dictionary for the vocabulary words.
* Have students play Vocabulary Concentration. The goal of this game is to match vocabulary words with their pictures. Divide the class into groups of two to five students. Have students make two sets of cards the same size and color. On one set, have them write the vocabulary words. On the second set, have them draw or cut out and paste pictures of each type of transportation. All cards are mixed together and placed face down on a table. A player picks two cards. If the pair matches the word with its definition, the player keeps the cards and takes another turn. If the cards do not match, they are returned to their places face down on the table, and another player takes a turn. Players must concentrate to remember the locations of the words and their pictures. The game continues until all matches have been made.

Curriculum Connections

You may wish to use one or all of the following activities to supplement your own ideas about ways to integrate the *Celebrate Our Similarities* theme into your curriculum.

Language Arts:

1. Have everyone in the class contribute to a story that tells what life would be like without wheels. After the class has completed the story, have students draw illustrations for it.

2. Show students pictures of trains. Have each student paint a small, empty box to look like the car on a train. Ask students to write their names on the sides of the boxes. Attach the boxes to a bulletin board to make a train.

Science:

1. Discuss how friction affects the way things move. Set up some experiments related to friction. For example: Pour water into two shallow bowls. Place a rubber ball in one bowl and a tennis ball in the other bowl. Have students try to move each ball. Ask them which one is easier to move. Discuss how a smooth surface is easier to move than a rough surface. Explain that many types of transportation have smooth surfaces so that they can move faster.

2. Have students draw a diagram of a bicycle. Provide an outline.

Social Studies:

1. Have students brainstorm a list of different types of transportation. Some examples include: bicycles, boats, cars, horses, motorcycles, planes, etc. Write your brainstorm on butcher paper and add to the list as you learn more.

2. Have students make a chart showing the types of transportation that use machinery (i.e., cars, planes, boats) and types that do not use machinery (i.e., gliders, horses, sailboats).

Math:

1. Have students use a route map to compute simple math problems while using mileage markers.

2. Ask students to conduct a survey to find out how students usually get to school. Have them graph the information collected.

Literature:

1. Read aloud to students the folk tale about John Henry. Discuss how new types of transportation can have benefits, such as making it easier and faster to travel from place to place, as well as problems, such as increasing amount of pollution.

2. Select stories related to transportation. See bibliography (page 174) for some suggestions. Record the stories on cassette tape and place them in a listening center for everyone to enjoy.

Art:

1. Have students make a mobile, using pictures they cut out and paste or pictures they draw of different types of transportation. Have students make three distinct parts on the mobile in order to separate the types of transportation: land, water, and air.

2. Have students draw a mural of transportation from around the world.

Life Skills:

1. Invite a guest speaker to class, to discuss different careers available in transportation.

2. Arrange to take students on a field trip to the local DMV.

Everybody Uses Transportation!

Transportation Chart

Directions: Read the words in the box. The words name things that people use to travel on the land, in the air, or in the water. Write each word under the correct heading. The first one is done for you.

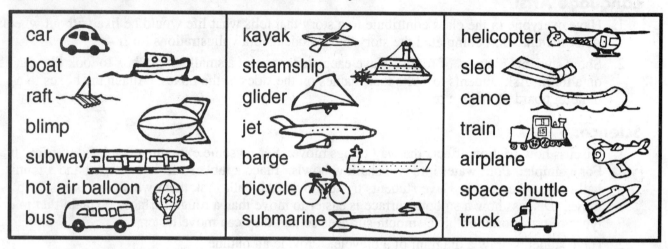

Land	Water	Air
1. __car__	1. _____	1. _____
2. _____	2. _____	2. _____
3. _____	3. _____	3. _____
4. _____	4. _____	4. _____
5. _____	5. _____	5. _____
6. _____	6. _____	6. _____
7. _____	7. _____	7. _____

What type of transportation would you most like to try? Explain your answer.

_____

_____

_____

Car Model

Many people around the world travel using a car. In this activity, you will make a model car that uses magnets to move.

Materials:

- 1 matchbox (empty)
- 2 bar magnets
- modeling clay
- plastic tape quarter
- 2 toothpicks
- 1 drinking straw
- 1 index card
- scissors
- 1 quarter or an object about the size of a

Directions:

Step 1: Open the matchbox. Place one bar magnet in the tray part of the matchbox and tape it down. Close the matchbox.

Step 2: Use scissors to cut two pieces of the drinking straw that are as long as the width of the matchbox.

Step 3: Use tape to attach the pieces of straw to the outside of the matchbox.

Step 4: Place a toothpick inside each piece of straw.

Step 5: Trace the quarter on the index card four times. Cut out the circles.

Step 6: Stick each end of the toothpicks through a circle to make the wheels.

Step 7: Hold the wheels in place by pressing a small piece of clay onto the point of each toothpick.

Step 8: Place the car on its wheels. Hold the other bar magnet in front of the car. Does the car move toward or away from the bar magnet?

Step 9: Turn the bar magnet around and hold it in front of the car again. Which way does the car move now?

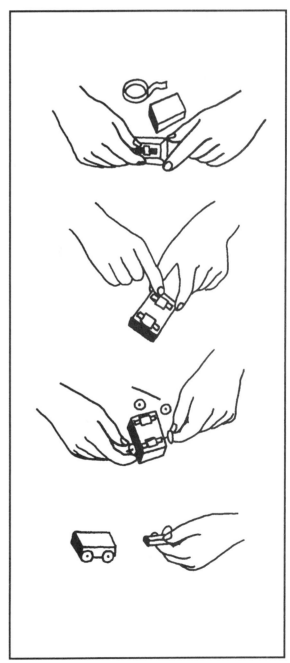

Canoe Model

Canoes were once used by many Native Americans. They built the frame out of wood. Then they covered the frame with bark from a birch tree. Finally they covered the bark with the sap from a pine or spruce tree. This kept water from leaking into the canoe.

Directions: Use the pattern shown below to make a model of a canoe. Cut out the pattern. Then trace it onto light brown construction paper. Use a black marker to decorate your canoe with different designs. Then fold your canoe on the dotted line and tape it together. Write a short poem about what you think it would be like to ride in a canoe.

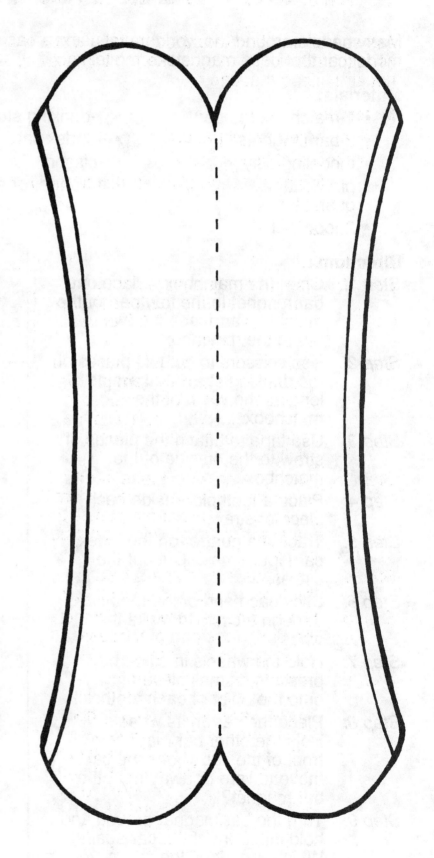

Model of a Hot Air Balloon

Ask students if they would like to take a ride in a hot air balloon. Have them tell what they think it would be like. In this activity, students will make a model of a hot air balloon that can fly.

Materials:

- enlarged panel pattern
- pieces of tissue paper
- a strip of tagboard glued in the shape of a ring
- a small box
- thread
- scissors
- ruler
- paintbrush
- glue
- hairdryer

Directions:

Step 1: Use an opaque projector to enlarge the panel pattern shown here. It should be 2-3 feet (60-90 cm) in length.

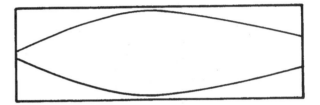

Step 2: Have students use the pattern to cut out eight panels from pieces of tissue paper. Warn students to be careful when handling the tissue paper because it tears easily.

Step 3: Have students glue together the edges of the panels. Have them glue the bottoms of the panels to the tagboard ring. Allow the glue to dry.

Step 4: Have students make a hole in the top corners of the small box.

Step 5: Have students carefully connect the box to the ring of tagboard, using pieces of thread.

Step 6: Have students place their balloons over a hairdryer, as shown here. Ask them to check to be sure the hairdryer is set to blow warm air. Then have them hold onto their balloons and turn on the hairdryer. Tell them to wait until each balloon has been filled up with warm air. Then have them let go of the balloons and watch them float into the air.

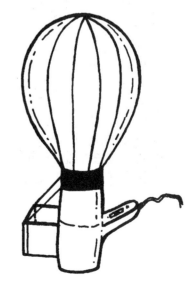

A Speed Boat Race

Follow the directions shown below to race a speed boat in a bowl of water.

Materials:

- index card or tagboard
- ruler
- scissors
- large plastic bowl
- liquid soap used for washing dishes

Directions:

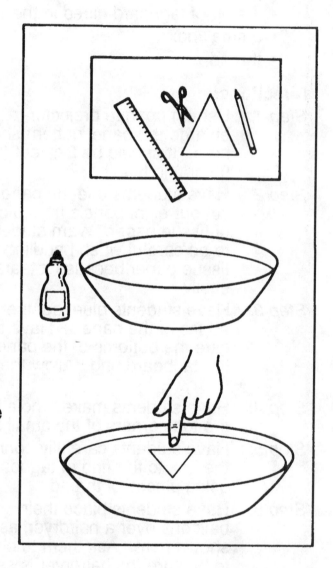

Step 1: To make your boat, use your ruler to draw the shape of a triangle on the index card or tagboard. The triangle can be any size.

Step 2: Use scissors to cut out your boat.

Step 3: Pour clean water into the bowl until it is about half full. Place your boat on the water. Your boat should float.

Step 4: Pour a little bit of liquid soap on one finger.

Step 5: Stick the finger with the soap into the water so that it is close to the back of your boat.

Step 6: Watch to see what happens to the boat.

Step 7: If you want to race your boat again, you will need to pour out the water you just used and replace it with clean water.

Transportation of the Future

Directions: Use the space below to draw a picture of a way you think people will travel in the future.

Everybody Goes to School!

Bulletin Board Idea

Use the following bulletin board idea to introduce the section on schools. The pattern shown below makes the bulletin board quick and easy to create. Begin by taking photographs of your students or by having them bring photographs of themselves from home. Cover the background of the bulletin board with butcher paper or fabric. Then use an opaque projector to enlarge and copy the pattern of the school bus that is shown below. Place the photographs in the windows of the bus. Finally, create the title "Everybody Goes to School!" You may also wish to place a table in front of the bulletin board to create a learning/research center to help students find out more about schools.

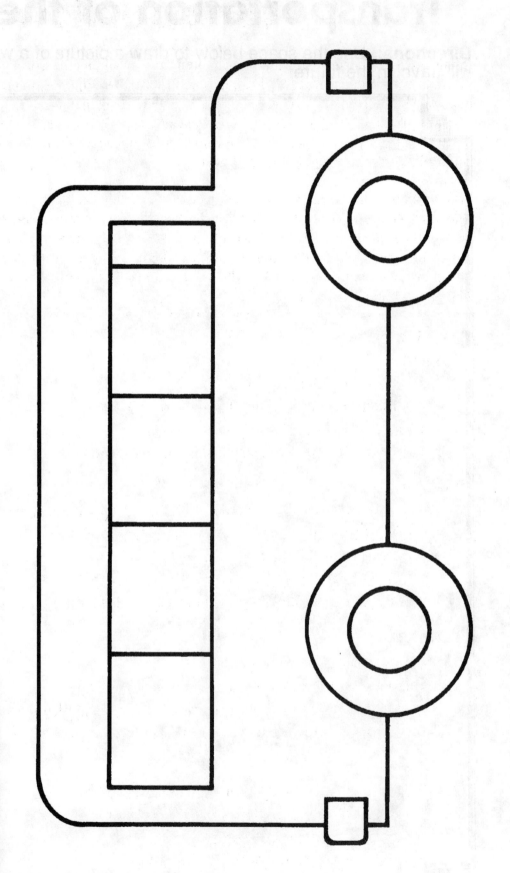

Introduction

In this section, students will learn that children from all around the world go to school. They will see that many of the things that they learn in school, such as reading, writing, and arithmetic, are also important subjects in other countries. They will understand that there are many important reasons for going to school. School activities give students the opportunity to learn skills that will be needed throughout their lives, prepare them for careers as adults, make them more responsible citizens, and help them recognize their abilities and interests.

Schools around the world vary, depending on the economic conditions of a country. Most industrialized nations have well-established school systems. Leaders in these countries understand that they need educated citizens if they want to be competitive in the world market. As a result, education is a priority, and children are required to go to school. However, many underdeveloped countries cannot afford to build and maintain schools. Due to lack of education, it will be difficult for change to take place in these countries.

Sample Plans

Lesson 1

- Introduce the section on schools.
- Brainstorm a list of activities that are done at school.
- Display books that tell stories about school.
- Display the school bus on a bulletin board (page 90).

Lesson 2

- Introduce the vocabulary related to schools; then do a vocabulary activity (page 92).
- Select activities from Curriculum Connections (page 93).
- Read *This Is the Way We Go to School* (page 94).
- Choose activities for *This Is the Way We Go to School* (page 94).
- Tell about experiences with going to school in other cities, states, or countries.

Lesson 3

- Do a vocabulary activity (page 92).
- Select activities from Curriculum Connections (page 93).
- Make a cone that German students make for carrying goodies (page 95).
- Construct a Chinese counting frame called an abacus (page 96).

Lesson 4

- Select activities from Curriculum Connections (page 93).
- Make a bookmark like the kind Japanese students use (page 97).
- Write a daily schedule on a chart (page 98).
- Answer some questions about school (page 99).

Background Information

Children from all around the world attend school. Countries such as the U.S., Japan, Australia, and Canada, as well as many European countries, emphasize the importance of education and have spent time, resources, and money establishing excellent school systems. These countries provide highly qualified teachers, educational materials, and technology needed for effective instruction.

Some countries have poorly developed school systems or no schools at all. The major concern of people living in these countries is not education, but rather the constant struggle to survive from one day to the next. These people are extremely poor and must spend what little money they do have on basic necessities such as food, shelter, and clothing. They cannot afford to pay teacher salaries, buy school supplies, or build schools.

From a historical perspective, the idea of having public schools is relatively new. Before the 1800s, most people did not go to school. Only an elite few, usually male children of wealthy landowners or children training to enter the priesthood, were able to attend a school. However, by the 1800s, many people came to realize that education was essential to a country's progress. As a result, free public education was established.

Vocabulary

You may wish to introduce the following vocabulary words at the beginning of this section: school, assignments, subjects, schedule, reading, writing, mathematics, language arts, social studies, history, geography, science, health, music, art, physical education.

Vocabulary Activities

You can help your students learn and retain the above vocabulary by providing them with interesting vocabulary activities. Here are a few ideas to try.

- Have students work in cooperative learning groups to write a story using as many of the vocabulary words as possible.

- Have the class play Twenty Clues. In this game, one student selects a vocabulary word and gives up to twenty clues (one at a time) about this word until someone in the class can guess it.

- Have students play a form of Concentration with their vocabulary words. The goal of this game is to have students match the vocabulary words with their definitions. Divide the class into small groups. Have students make two sets of cards that are the same size and color. On one set of cards, have them write the vocabulary words. On the other set of cards, have them write the definitions or use the words in sentences. All of the cards are mixed together and placed face down on the table or floor. A player picks two cards. If the pair matches the definition with the word, the player keeps the cards and takes another turn. If the pair does not match, the cards are returned face down to their places and the next player takes a turn. It is important for players to remember the locations of the words and their definitions. Students should continue to play until all of the matches have been made.

- Write sentences, leaving blanks where the vocabulary words belong. Ask students to use context clues to complete the sentences.

92

Curriculum Connections

You may wish to use one or all of the following activities to supplement your own ideas about ways to integrate the *Celebrate Our Similarities* theme into your curriculum.

Language Arts:

1. Have students make a chart with the following headings: likes, dislikes. Then have students make a list of things they like and dislike about school. Ask students to share some of their likes and dislikes.

2. Ask students to write adventure stories that take place in a school. Have them illustrate their stories. Then display the stories in the hallway for everyone to enjoy.

Science:

1. Discuss the concept of environmental pollution. Ask students to draw posters that show what they can do to help keep their school clean. Ask how the school can help the community become more environmentally conscious. For example, students could work to organize a recycling program so that people in the community have a place to drop off cans, newspapers, etc.

2. Have students brainstorm a list of science-related topics. Then have them take a poll to see which topics are the most interesting to the class and show the results in a graph or table.

Social Studies:

1. Have students brainstorm a list of tools that they use at school. Examples: pencils, pens, books, paper, crayons, erasers, scissors, glue, rulers, microscopes, globes, maps.

2. Have students discuss the purpose of having rules in the classroom. Ask them to explain what would happen if there were no rules. Have them apply this information to why society has laws for people to follow.

Math:

1. Have students create word problems that are school related. Students could practice basic math facts, how to add and subtract money, and how to calculate amounts of time.

2. Arrange to have students observe or help in the school cafeteria. For example, students could help with food preparation by measuring different ingredients for recipes.

Literature:

1. Have students read a story about school. See the bibliography (page 174) for suggestions. Then ask students to do a book report. The report can be written, oral, or both.

2. Divide the class into cooperative learning groups. Allow each group time in the school library. Have students work together to make a list of books that are about school. You may wish to have them create a chart that shows which books are fiction and which are nonfiction.

Art:

Have students draw and paint pictures of themselves doing their favorite school activities. Allow time for students to tell the class about their picture.

Life Skills:

1. Ask students how they get to and from school. Have them discuss safety rules that apply to pedestrians, bike riders, car riders, bus riders, etc.

2. Arrange to take students to different types of schools in your community. Examples: schools for the visually or hearing impaired, Montessori schools, magnet schools, etc.

Literature Connection

Title: *This Is the Way We Go to School*
Author: Edith Baer
Publisher: Scholastic (1990)

Summary: This story is written using rhyming couplets, and the illustrations are colorful cartoons. This format will appeal to children of all ages. The book tells how children go to school on each of the different continents. At the end of the book, a world map is provided on which each character's homeland is pinpointed.

Note: This book provides an excellent opportunity to connect the section on transportation to the section on schools in *Celebrate Our Similarities*.

Suggested Activities:

1. Have students suggest what the book will be about by looking at the cover and title.

2. Discuss with students how they get to and from school. Ask students whether they get to and from school like any of the characters in the story.

3. Ask students to identify the rhyming words in the story.

4. Have students discuss how schools might be the same no matter where they are in the world.

5. Have students add new pages to their books that show how they get to school. Ask them to write rhyming couplets to go along with their illustrations.

6. Ask students to use small pieces of construction paper to make mosaics that show something about school. They might choose to show a school building, a school activity, or children on their way to school.

7. Provide copies of the world map (page 173). Help students locate the countries that are mentioned in the book. Then have them color those countries on their maps.

8. Take photographs of children actively involved in school activities. Display the photographs on a bulletin board.

9. Have students write descriptions of their classroom. Allow time for students to share their descriptions with the class.

10. Divide the class into cooperative learning groups. Ask students to brainstorm a list of ways to make someone who has just arrived at their school feel welcome.

11. Have students role-play different ways to get to and from school. You may also wish to have them role-play different activities that they do during the school day.

12. Discuss the different types of careers available in a school. Then invite faculty members, such as the principal, secretary, and counselor, to speak to your class about their jobs. Have students work with partners to make a list of questions they want to ask before each guest comes to visit.

13. Ask students to tell how they think children living in the future will get to and from school. Have them draw illustrations that show this method of transportation.

14. Have students make a chart with the following headings: land, water, air. Under the appropriate headings, have students list the ways that children in the story get to school.

German Paper Cone

When children in Germany go to school for the very first time, they are given a large cone made out of paper. The cone is decorated by the parents. Then it is filled with tasty snacks for the first day of school.

Follow the directions shown below to make a small cone.

Materials:
- scissors stickers,
- cone pattern
- glue
- tagboard
- a snack, such as nuts or raisins
- crayons, markers, wrapping paper, glitter, fabric, or wrapping paper
- tape
- stapler

Directions:

Step 1: Cut out the pattern shown here.

Step 2: Glue it onto a piece of tagboard. Allow the glue to dry. Then cut out the pattern again.

Step 3: Decorate your cone with crayons, markers, wrapping paper, stickers, glitter, fabric, wrapping paper, or anything else you like.

Step 4: Carefully roll the tagboard into the shape of a cone. Tape the cone in place.

Step 5: Cut a strip of tagboard to use as a handle. Be sure it is long enough before you put it on the cone. Then staple it in place.

Step 6: Pour your snack into the cone. Then share your snack with a friend.

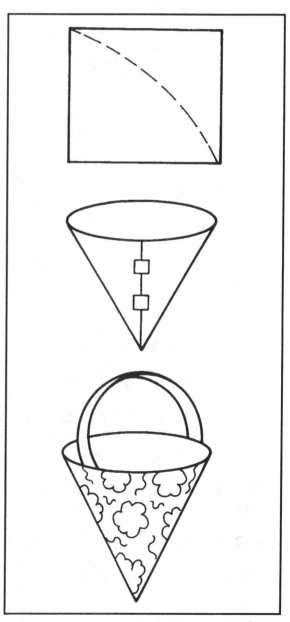

Chinese Abacus

Children in China learn how to use an abacus. An abacus is a tool that can be used to count numbers. In this activity, you will make an abacus.

Materials:

- picture frame, with the picture removed
- string or yarn
- ruler
- thumbtacks
- beads or macaroni noodles

Directions:

Step 1: Measure the length of the picture frame with the string. Add 3" (7.5 cm) more to the length of the string. Then cut three more pieces of string that length.

Step 2: On each end of the frame, put in four thumbtacks that are the same distance apart.

Step 3: Tie one string to a thumbtack. Place seven beads on that string. Then tie the other end of the string to the thumbtack on the opposite side of the picture frame.

Repeat this with the other three strings. Be sure that the strings do not cross over each other.

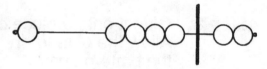

Step 4: Hold the frame so that the strings go from side to side. Push five of the beads on each string to the left. Push two of the beads on each string to the right.

Step 5: Cut a piece of string that is two times longer than the strings you cut in Step 1. Place two thumbtacks, one at the top of the frame and one at the bottom as shown here.

Step 6: Tie the long piece of string to the thumbtack on the top. Tie a knot each time you cross one of the five strings.

Now the abacus is ready to use. Here is how much each bead is worth.

Here is what the number 143 looks like.

Now try another one on your own.

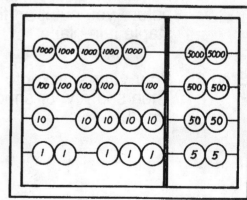

96

Japanese Bookmark

Origami, or paper folding, is one type of activity Japanese children enjoy. In this activity you will learn how to use origami to make a bookmark that looks like a leaf.

Materials:

- square pattern
- crayons or markers
- scissors

Directions:

Step 1: Use crayons or markers to decorate the square pattern shown here. Then cut it out.

Step 2: Fold the square in half from corner to corner.

Step 3: Fold down the top triangle.

Step 4: Flip over the paper. Fold down the middle flap.

Step 5: Fold three corners as shown here.

Step 6: Turn the bookmark over and place it in a book.

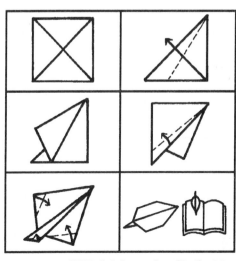

Your Day at School

What kinds of things do you do at school? Think about all the subjects that you study. Think about all the types of activities that you do.

Directions: Look at the sample schedule shown below. Then use the form at the bottom of the page to make a schedule of your day at school. First write the time and subject. Remember to write A.M. for times in the morning and P.M. for times in the afternoon. Then name one or more things that you are learning about in each subject.

Sample Schedule

Name: LaShanda Moore   Teacher: Ms. Grant
Date: Nov. 12, 1996   Room: 205

Time	Subject	Activity
8:00 - 9:00 A.M.	Math	Addition
9:00 - 9:30 A.M.	Art	Drawing

Your Schedule

Name: Teacher:
Date: Room:

Time	Subject	Activity

Everybody Goes to School!

Questions About School

Directions: Use complete sentences to answer the questions about school.

1. What is the name of your school?_____

2. What is your teacher's name?_____

3. What grade are you in? _____

4. How many students are in your class? _____

5. How do you get to and from school each day?_____

6. What time does school start each day? _____

7. What time does school end each day? _____

8. Which subject do you like the best? Tell why. _____

   _____

9. Which subject do you like the least? Tell why. _____

   _____

10. What is your favorite game to play at school? Tell why. _____

    _____

11. What kind of books do you like to check out from your school library? _____

    _____

12. What is one thing you have already learned about this year? _____

    _____

13. What is one thing you would like to learn about this year?_____

    _____

14. What is one thing you hope never changes at your school? _____

    _____

15. What is one thing you would like to change at your school? _____

    _____

Bulletin Board Idea

Use the following bulletin board idea to introduce the section on stories. The pattern shown below makes the bulletin board quick and easy to create. Begin by covering the background with butcher paper. Then use an opaque projector to enlarge and copy the book pattern shown below. Place the book in the middle of the bulletin board. Hang a small world map on the left-hand page of the book. Then create the title "Stories from Around the World." Place the title on the right-hand page of the book. Use the rest of the bulletin board to display covers from a variety of books that contain stories from around the world. You may also wish to place a table in front of the bulletin board to create a learning/research center to help students find out more about stories from around the world.

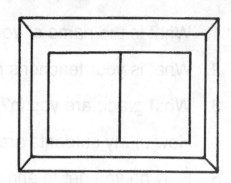

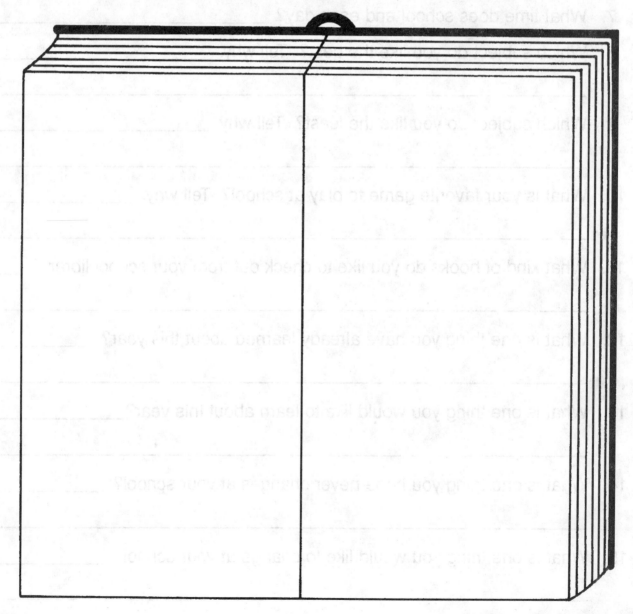

Introduction

People of all ages from all over the world enjoy stories. The first stories were told orally. They were passed down from generation to generation in this way. Later people began to develop a system of writing. As a result, they learned to write their stories in books. This meant that these stories could be enjoyed by more and more people. By the 1500s, people from different countries were able to travel from place to place with greater ease. Some people decided to settle in colonies that were being established in the New World. Other people were captured as slaves and forcibly taken to places far away from their homeland. Wherever these people went, whether they got there by choice or not, they took their stories with them. Often the stories of one culture were borrowed by another. Sometimes stories were changed by the people who told them to reflect the change in environment.

Today, most people read stories in books or listen to them on cassette tapes. Many people find both of these an enjoyable and relaxing way to experience a story. However, some people still enjoy practicing the art of storytelling. These people believe that the feeling that goes with the story is lost when it is read from a printed page. Storytellers make the characters, setting, and story events come alive for the listener. Sometimes they use props, but usually storytellers rely on their voices, facial expressions, and body movements to entertain their audiences. Many people find it fascinating that a storyteller never tells a story exactly the same way twice.

Sample Plans

Lesson 1

- Introduce the section on stories.
- Display the bulletin board (page 100).
- Discuss what types of stories are enjoyed the most.
- Keep a reading log as a variety of stories from different countries are read.

Lesson 2

- Introduce the vocabulary for the stories people enjoy; then do a vocabulary activity (page 102).
- Select activities from Curriculum Connections (page 103).
- Discuss the meanings of story elements (characters, setting, plot).
- Read and discuss *The Magic Pot* (page 104).
- Retell *The Magic Pot* by showing the major events of the story (page 105).

Lesson 3

- Do a vocabulary activity (page 102).
- Select activities from Curriculum Connections (page 103).
- Read *Jack and the Beanstalk* (page 106).
- Make a mobile that tells the story elements for *Jack and the Beanstalk* (page 107).

Lesson 4

- Select activities from Curriculum Connections (page 103).
- Use a Venn diagram to compare *The Magic Pot* and *Jack and the Beanstalk* (page 108).
- Take a poll to see which story, *The Magic Pot* or *Jack and the Beanstalk,* was liked more.
- Write a new ending for *The Magic Pot* or *Jack and the Beanstalk* (page 109).

Background Information

Stories that are shared by people in a particular culture are usually considered part of folklore. These stories are told by each generation so that the next generation will know them. Myths, folk tales, and legends make up the kinds of stories told in folklore.

Myths

Some stories are of a religious nature. These are called myths. They are often used to explain how things such as the world and people got to be the way they are. For example, some myths tell how the earth was created while others are used to describe how people came to inhabit the earth. The people who created the myths believed that they were describing what really happened.

Folk Tales

Folk tales, which are stories about animals or humans, include fables and fairy tales. Fables are fictional stories about animals who have human-like characteristics. They are always intended to teach a lesson. Fairy tales can be about humans and their struggles, or they can be about animals who behave like humans. Folk tales are extremely popular with people of all ages.

Legends

Legends, although set in the more recent past, are similar to myths because they can be used to describe how things came to be. However, they are also often used to tell about the deeds of heroes and heroines. As was the case with myths, the people who created legends thought that they were telling true stories.

Vocabulary

You may wish to introduce the following vocabulary words at the beginning of this section: folk tale, fairy tale, fable, legend, myth, story, fiction, nonfiction, biography, autobiography.

Vocabulary Activities

You can help your students learn and retain the above vocabulary by providing them with interesting vocabulary activities. Here are a few ideas to try.

- Have students use these words as their weekly spelling list.
- Before students enter the classroom, hide index cards around the room, some with vocabulary words written on them and others with definitions on them. When the class arrives, divide them into two teams to play Vocabulary Hide and Seek. Allow students to search the room for a period of time that you designate. Teams can score a point by matching a word with its definition. The winning team is the one with the most points at the end of the time period.
- Have students make Word Scrambles by writing each vocabulary word with the letters rearranged on a 4" x 2" (10 cm x 5 cm) piece of construction paper. On the back of each piece of paper, have students write the word as it is correctly spelled. Then divide the class into two teams. Have students compete to unscramble the words and give meanings for them. Award one point for each correct answer. The winning team is the one with the most points at the end of a period of time designated by you.

Curriculum Connections

You may wish to use one or all of the following activities to supplement your own ideas about ways to integrate the *Celebrate Our Similarities* theme into your curriculum.

Language Arts:

1. Read a story with students. Ask the class to work together to write a summary of the story.

2. Introduce the elements of a story (characters, setting, plot). Ask students to identify these elements in the stories they read.

3. Write *Author's Purpose* on the chalkboard. Explain to students that an author's purpose is the reason she or he wrote a story. Tell them that stories can be written for such reasons as to inform, entertain, teach a lesson, or persuade. As students read different stories, ask them to identify the author's purpose.

Social Studies:

1. Have students use a map or globe to locate the origin of each story that the class reads.

2. Help students make a chart that names five countries. Have them write three to five titles of stories that originated in each of those countries.

Example:

France	England	Denmark	Norway	Russia
Cinderella	*Jack and the Beanstalk*	*The Magic Pot*	*The Three Billy Goats Gruff*	*The Flying Ship*

Math:

1. Divide the class into cooperative learning groups. Provide each group with a book that contains multiple stories. Have students use the table of contents to determine the length of each story in the book.

2. Read aloud a story from another country. Have students make up problems that are related to the content of a story.

Literature:

1. Read aloud a story from another country. See the bibliography (page 174) for a list of suggested books that contain stories from other countries. Then have students rewrite the story from another character's point of view.

2. For one or two weeks, have students keep a reading log that shows the titles and authors of stories they have read or that have been read to them.

Art:

1. After students read a story, have them create puppets for the main characters in the story. Then ask them to tell how they made their puppets.

2. Read a story with students. Have them create a mural that shows scenes from the story.

3. Read aloud a story to the class, but do not show any of the illustrations. Ask students to draw their own illustrations to go with the story.

Life Skills:

Read a story with students. Then divide the class into cooperative learning groups. Have the groups decide which part of the story they liked best. Ask students to organize and present a skit about their favorite part of the story.

The Magic Pot

(a story from Denmark)

Once there was a poor man and his wife living in a tiny house. They did not have enough money for food so they decided to sell their cow.

The next day, the man got up very early and started walking to town with the cow. As he went down the road, the man saw a stranger. The stranger asked if the cow was for sale. The man said he was selling the cow for $100. The stranger said he did not have any money but that he could trade something for the cow. He showed the man a large pot. The stranger explained that the pot was magic. Just as the man was about to say he did not want the pot, it began to talk. It said, "Take me home with you." The man could not believe his ears. He knew this really was a magic pot, so he traded the cow for it and headed home.

When the man got home, he told his wife about trading the cow. The woman was not happy and did not believe that the pot was magic. Suddenly the pot began to talk. The woman was very surprised, and she knew that her husband had been right. This really was a magic pot! The pot told the woman to start a fire for cooking, so she did. Then it started dancing around. The woman asked, "Where are you going?" The pot said that it was going to the greedy rich man's house, and it danced away. A short time later the pot returned, and it was full of food. The couple ate well, and they were very happy.

The next day the pot began to dance again. The woman asked, "Where are you going?" The pot said that it was going to the greedy rich man's shed, and then it danced away. In a little while, the pot returned. This time it came back full of wheat. The poor couple had never seen so much wheat! They knew they would be able to eat for years with all of that wheat.

The very next day, the pot began to dance again. The woman asked, "Where are you going?" The pot replied that it was going to get the gold that the greedy rich man had buried, and then it danced away. When the pot returned, it was full of gold. The man and the woman were amazed. They couldn't believe they were rich.

Later that day, the pot began to dance once more for the couple. The woman asked, "Where are you going?" This time the pot told her that it was going to take the greedy rich man to the North Pole. Then the pot danced away, going in the direction of the greedy man's house. The man and his wife never saw the magic pot again, but they were always thankful for all of the wonderful things it had given them.

After you have read the story, do the activity on page 105.

Retell the Story

Make a book that shows what happened in *The Magic Pot,* page 104.

Materials:
- 3 pieces of paper 8 1/2 inches (22 cm) by 11 inches (28 cm)
- ruler
- crayons or markers
- stapler

Directions:

Step 1: Place the pieces of paper on top of each other so that all three can be seen.

Step 2: Carefully fold over the top of each piece of paper. Now you should be able to see all three at the top.

Step 3: Staple across the top close to where the pages are folded. Then turn the book so that the fold is on your left.

Step 4: Write the title "The Magic Pot" on the top page. Number the other pages 1 through 5.

Step 5: Pick five of the most important events from the story. On each page draw a picture and write a couple of sentences to tell about one of these events. Be sure you use only one event on each page.

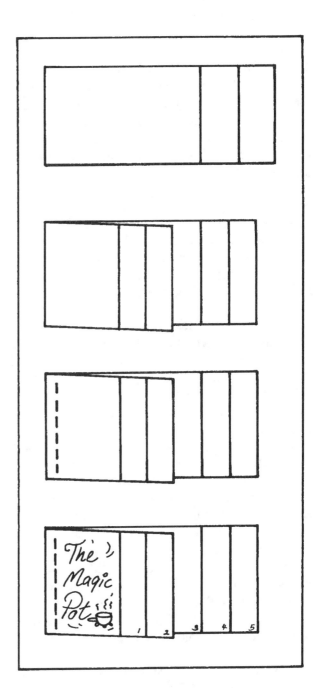

Jack and the Beanstalk

(a story from England)

Once there was a poor widow and her son, Jack, living in a small cabin. They got a little money to buy food by selling milk from their cow. Then one day the cow stopped giving any milk. The widow told Jack to take the cow to town and sell her.

The next day, Jack headed toward town with the cow. On his way, Jack met a stranger who asked him to trade the cow for five magic beans. Jack took the beans and gave the cow to the stranger. When Jack got home, he told his mother about trading the cow for the beans. Jack's mother was angry. She tossed the beans out the window and sent Jack to bed without any dinner.

The next morning Jack woke up and saw a huge beanstalk outside the cabin. The beans really were magic! Jack ran outside and climbed the beanstalk. When he got to the clouds, he saw a road and followed it until he came to a tall woman standing outside of a large house. Jack asked the woman for some food since he was very hungry. The woman told Jack that he might **be food** if her husband, the giant, found him at the house! But the woman felt sorry for Jack, so she took him into the kitchen and gave him some food.

Suddenly the giant came home. Jack had just enough time to hide inside the oven. The giant said he could smell a boy. Then he promised to eat any boy that he found. The giant's wife told him to stop daydreaming and sit down to eat. So the giant sat and ate. After eating, the giant took out two sacks filled with gold. As he counted the gold, the giant fell asleep. Jack jumped out of the oven and grabbed a sack of gold. He went home as fast as he could and gave the gold to his mother.

A few days later, Jack climbed the beanstalk again and hid inside the giant's house. The giant sat down to eat. This time he felt sure he could smell a boy and repeated his promise to eat any boy he found. The giant's wife told him to eat and stop being so silly. After eating, the giant put a hen on the table and told it to lay some golden eggs. While the hen laid her eggs, the giant fell asleep. Jack grabbed the hen, took it home, and showed his mother how it could lay beautiful golden eggs.

Not long after taking the hen, Jack went up the beanstalk and hid inside the giant's house once more. The giant was eating, when Jack heard him say that he could smell a boy. As the giant looked around, he again promised to eat any boy he found. But Jack was well hidden, and the giant did not see him. After eating, the giant took out a golden harp and told it to play. The lovely music that came from the harp put the giant to sleep. Just as Jack was grabbing the harp, the giant woke up and was very angry! He followed Jack, who was running with the harp to the beanstalk. As Jack began climbing down the beanstalk, so did the giant. Jack yelled to his mother to bring an ax, which she did. After Jack got to the ground, he used the ax to chop down the beanstalk and the giant fell to his death. Now Jack and his mother were safe from the giant. They were also very happy and rich now that they had a bag filled with gold, a hen that laid golden eggs, and a golden harp.

After you have read the story, do the activity on page 107.

106

A Story Mobile

Directions: Reread *Jack and the Beanstalk* on page 106. Draw pictures and write sentences that tell the characters, setting, and at least four major events from the story. Cut out the pieces of the mobile. Then use a hanger and string to put the mobile together.

JACK AND THE BEANSTALK

Characters: ○	Setting: ○
Event 1: ○	Event 4: ○
Event 2: ○	Event 5: ○
Event 3: ○	Event 6: ○

Venn Diagram

Directions: Reread *The Magic Pot* (page 104) and *Jack and the Beanstalk* (page 106). Think about the things that are the same in the stories. Think about the things that are different. Use the Venn diagram below to tell how the stories are the same

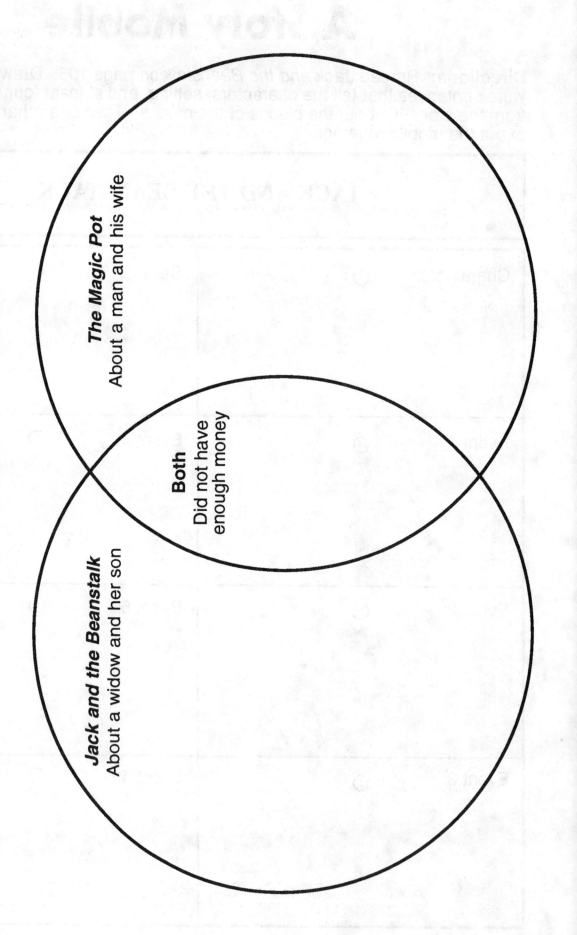

The Magic Pot
About a man and his wife

Both
Did not have
enough money

Jack and the Beanstalk
About a widow and her son

A New Ending

Directions: Pick one of the stories, *The Magic Pot* (page 104) or *Jack and the Beanstalk* (page 106). Reread that story. What is another way the story could end? Write a new ending for the story on this page.

_____

_____

_____

_____

_____

_____

_____

_____

_____

_____

_____

_____

_____

_____

_____

_____

_____

_____

_____

Bulletin Board Idea

Use the following bulletin board idea to introduce the section on games and toys. The patterns shown below make the bulletin board quick and easy to create. Begin by covering the background with butcher paper. Then use an opaque projector to enlarge and copy the patterns shown below. Finally, create the title "Games and Toys." You may also wish to place a table in front of the bulletin board to create a learning/research center to help students find out more about games and toys.

Introduction

Games and toys are enjoyed by children all around the world. In this section, students will learn that many of the games and toys they are familiar with are very similar to the games and toys children in other parts of the world have. When comparing games that are similar, students will note that the rules, playing areas, or game pieces might be a little different from those they are accustomed to. However, the basic premise of the game will remain the same. For example, as students read the Literature Connection for this section, *Hopscotch Around the World,* they will have the opportunity to see how the game of hopscotch is played in different countries. When comparing toys, students will see that the same kind of toy can be made using a variety of different materials.

Sample Plans

Lesson 1
- Introduce the section on games and toys.
- Set up a display that includes both games and toys.
- Brainstorm two lists, one of games and the other of toys.
- Display the games and toys bulletin board (page 110).

Lesson 2
- Introduce the vocabulary for games and toys (page 112).
- Select activities from Curriculum Connections (page 113).
- Read *Hopscotch Around the World* (page 114).
- Choose activities for *Hopscotch Around the World* (page 114).

Lesson 3
- Do a vocabulary activity (page 112).
- Select activities from Curriculum Connections (page 113).
- Use buttons to make a Greek yo-yo (page 115).
- Learn how to play the German game of Nine Pins (page 116).

Lesson 4
- Select activities from Curriculum Connections (page 113).
- Make a Daruma doll from Japan (page 117).
- Learn the rules for how to play Cheetah, Cheetal, a game from India (page 118).

Lesson 5
- Select activities from Curriculum Connections (page 113).
- Make up rules for your own game.
- Play with Native American stick dice (page 119).
- Learn the rules for how to play a Native American pebble game (page 119).

Lesson 6
- Select activities from Curriculum Connections (page 117).
- Make a Jewish top called a dreidel and learn how to play the dreidel game (120).
- Draw a picture of a favorite game or toy (page 121).

Background Information

Toys

Children have played with toys since ancient times. In Egypt, balls, carved animals, and pull toys were popular. In Greece and Rome, children played with hoops, hobbyhorses, cars, and boats. In China and Japan, children everywhere were spinning tops. During the Middle Ages, puppets and rattles became the favorite toys of European children. Some children became very innovative and created toys with objects they used in their everyday lives.

By the early 1900s, the toy industry in the United States was a huge success. Toys came in all shapes and sizes. Toy manufacturers began designing toys that were based on what children liked in addition to what was developmentally appropriate for each child's age.

Legislators became increasingly concerned that certain toys were unsafe for children. As a result they passed a law in 1969 that prevented the sale of toys that were made with poisonous ingredients, that were flammable, or that had surfaces that could cause injury.

Games

Games have probably always been an important part of human existence. In general, traditional games include target games, board games, tile games, word and picture games, card games, and fantasy and war games. In target games, each player has to throw something at a designated target. Marbles, horseshoes, and darts are examples of target games. In board games, players use markers, or game pieces, to move around the playing board. Checkers, Parcheesi, and backgammon are examples of board games. Tile games use tiles made out of materials which included wood, plastic, bone, or ivory. Dominoes and Scrabble are examples of tile games. Players of word and picture games must be able to use clues to determine an answer. An example of a word game is Twenty Questions. Card games refers to any of the hundreds of games played with a deck of playing cards. Rummy and poker are two card games. Fantasy and war games require players to use strategy and imagination to win. Dungeons and Dragons is an example of this type of game. Many traditional games are still played by children around the world. Since the 1970s, a new type of game that uses electronics has also become very popular.

Vocabulary

You may wish to introduce the following vocabulary words at the beginning of this section: toys, plays, games, rules, board games, tile games, war and fantasy games, target games, card games, word and picture games, electronic games.

Vocabulary Activities

You can help your students learn and retain the above vocabulary by providing them with interesting vocabulary activities. Here are a few ideas to try.

- Have students work in small groups to define the vocabulary words and record the words and their definitions in a class vocabulary notebook.

- Have students create alphables by listing the words in alphabetical order and dividing them into syllables.

Curriculum Connections

You may wish to use one or all of the following activities to supplement your own ideas about ways to integrate the *Celebrate Our Similarities* theme into your curriculum.

Language Arts:

1. Have students make a chart that has the headings "Games" and "Toys." Then ask them to brainstorm a list of games and toys they know and write them under the appropriate heading on the chart.

2. Display a variety of toys. Ask students to write descriptions of toys without naming them. Have them trade their descriptions with partners. Have the partners try to figure out which toy is being described.

3. Have students draw pictures that show games or toys they think children in the future might use. Ask them to write stories about children playing these games.

Science:

1. Have students use everyday materials to construct dolls. For example, students could use pieces of fabric, vegetables, or rocks to make dolls.

2. Ask students to bring from home toys that have moving parts. Then have them explain to the class how the toy works.

Social Studies:

1. Have students explain the importance of having rules for games. Lead them to conclude that if games did not have rules, they would be disorganized and would probably not be very enjoyable to play.

2. Have students create a time line that shows when different toys and/or games from around the world were invented. Display the time line along the classroom wall.

3. Have students write letters to toy or game manufacturers. Have students ask for information about how the companies got started.

Math:

1. Have students use rulers to determine the dimensions for different toys and games. For example, students could measure the length and width of playing boards and playing cards, or they could measure the height of a top or stuffed animal.

2. Have students bring a variety of tops to school. Have them use a scale to measure the weight of each top. Then ask students to arrange the tops in order from lightest to heaviest. This activity can also be done with other toys.

3. Take a poll to find out which toys or games are the most popular with students in your class. Then have students use that information to make graphs.

Art:

1. Provide newspaper advertisements and catalogs from toy stores for students to use to cut out pictures. Have students make collages of games and toys, using the pictures that they cut out.

2. Have students make mosaics that show toys.

Life Skills:

Arrange to take students on a field trip to a toy factory or toy store. After returning to school, discuss the trip with students. Then ask them to draw pictures of their favorite parts of the trip.

Literature Connection

> **Title:** *Hopscotch Around the World*
> **Author:** Mary D. Lankford
> **Publisher:** Morrow (1992)

Summary: This book is the result of the author's extensive research to find out about the different ways that hopscotch is played around the world. Hopscotch is an ancient game that was first played by the Romans. However, today different versions of the game can be found throughout the world. The book includes interesting facts, diagrams of patterns that are traced on the ground for nineteen versions of the game, and illustrations showing children from different countries playing hopscotch.

Suggested Activities:

1. Read the book aloud to students. Then display a wall map of the world and provide copies of the world map (page 173) for students to color. Use the wall map to help students locate each of the countries mentioned in the book. Then have them color those countries on their maps.

2. Each day take students outside to teach them how to play one of the different versions of hopscotch. Begin by using chalk to draw one of the hopscotch boards as described in the book. Then teach students the rules for that game of hopscotch. Have students learn at least four or five versions of the game.

3. Have students use pieces of fabric or construction paper to create miniature models of the different hopscotch boards that are described in the book. Display the models on a bulletin board.

4. Provide students with pieces of construction paper. Have them glue the pieces into the shape of a traditional hopscotch board. Ask students to use each part of the construction paper hopscotch board to draw or paint pictures of their favorite games.

5. Have students write a story that includes children playing one type of hopscotch.

6. Use chalk to draw a traditional hopscotch board on the sidewalk. To mark the spaces on the board, use skills that students are working on rather than just numerals. For example, each space could have addition or subtraction problems, number words, or reading vocabulary words. Then have students play the game and review needed skills at the same time.

7. Tell students that you want to add another section to the book. Have students work together to make up a new version of hopscotch.

8. Have students tell which versions of hopscotch are their favorites and explain why they liked that particular one.

9. Make a list of the nineteen types of hopscotch described in the book. Conduct a poll to see how many students like each type. Then have students use the data to make a graph.

10. Have students write poems about the fun of playing hopscotch.

11. Provide poster board for students. Have them create a class big book that shows the different types of hopscotch.

12. Provide copies of the world map (page 173). Have students pretend that they are visiting each of the countries mentioned in the book. Ask them to draw a line that shows the route they would take to get from place to place. Then have them tell what types of transportation they would use to make their trips.

A Yo-Yo from Greece

Follow the directions shown below to learn how to make a yo-yo like those used by Greek children.

Materials:

- two buttons that are 2 inches (5 cm) in diameter
- a paper clip that is 1 inch (2.5 cm) long
- 2 yards (1.8 meters) heavy-duty fishing line
- pieces of cardboard
- pliers
- wire cutters

Directions:

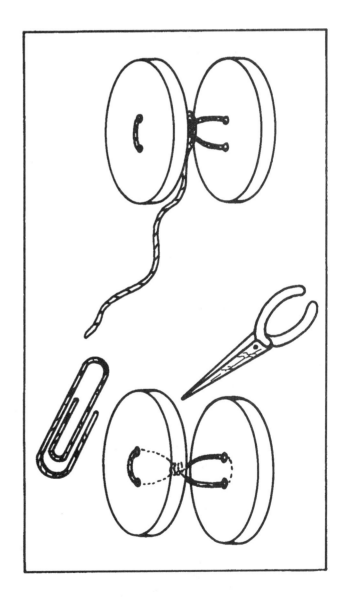

Step 1: Place the buttons with their backs together.

Step 2: Bend out each end of the paper clip so that it looks like an S. Poke the ends of the paper clip through the holes in the buttons.

Step 3: Slip some cardboard between the buttons to keep them about 1/4" (0.6 cm) apart. Use the pliers to twist the ends of the paper clip together between the buttons.

Step 4: Use wire cutters to cut off the ends of the paper clip. Then squeeze the twisted part of the paper clip with the pliers until it is flat.

Step 5: Hold one button in each hand. Twist the center of the paper clip by gently turning the buttons in opposite directions once or twice.

Step 6: Take out the pieces of cardboard. Tie the fishing line to the middle of the paper clip. Wrap the fishing line around the paper clip. Tie a loop that is big enough for two fingers at the end of the fishing line.

Nine Pins from Germany

Children in Germany like to play a game called Ninepins. This game was first played during the Middle Ages. It is a bowling game that uses a ball to knock down nine pins.

In this activity, you will work with three or four other students to make and play Ninepins.

Materials:

- 9 one-quart (0.95 liter) clean bleach or vinegar bottles
- permanent marker
- rubber ball, 7 inches (17.5 cm) in diameter

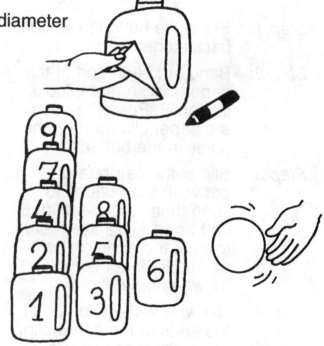

Directions:

Step 1: Peel off the labels from the bottles.

Step 2: Use a permanent marker to number the bottles from 1 to 9.

Step 3: Place the bottles as shown here.

Step 4: Now take turns rolling the ball to knock down the pins. For each turn, a player gets two chances to knock down all the pins. If a player knocks down all the pins with the first try, it is the next player's turn.

Step 5: Keep score by adding the numbers on the bottles that are knocked down each time.

Step 6: Continue playing until everyone has had ten turns. The winner is the person who has the most points at the end of the game. Who was the winner of the game your group played?_____

M A R Y	3	9	2	
B O B	4	6	7	

116   ©1995 Teacher Created Materials, Inc.

A Daruma Doll from Japan

The daruma doll is very popular throughout Japan. In this activity, you will make a daruma doll. Then try to tip it over and watch it sit up straight again.

Materials:

- half of a sponge ball that is 1-2 inches (2.5-5 cm) in diameter
- two pieces of construction paper, 4 inches by 6 inches (10 cm by 15 cm)
- masking tape, 1/2 inch (1.25 cm) wide
- glue
- paint or permanent markers

Directions:

Step 1: Cut out the cone pattern shown here.

Step 2: Trace the cone pattern onto the pieces of construction paper. Cut the patterns out of the construction paper.

Step 3: Roll the pieces of construction paper together to form a cone and glue them in place.

Step 4: Use the masking tape to hold the cone onto the ball.

Step 5: Draw or paint a face on the ball.

Step 6: Place your doll on a table or desk. Turn the point of the cone to spin the doll, or try to push it over to one side, and then let go.

Cheetah, Cheetal from India

Cheetah, Cheetal is a game played by children in India. It is a game of tag in which the cheetahs, a type of large cat, tries to catch the cheetals, a type of deer.

Materials:

- chalk or wide masking tape

Directions:

Step 1: Ask one student to be the leader. Then divide the rest of the class into two teams. There should be at least seven students on each team. Assign one team to be the cheetahs and the other team to be the cheetals.

Step 2: Measure a playing field that is about 20 feet (6 m) long. At each end of the playing field use chalk or masking tape to mark a base line.

Step 3: Place the teams in two separate lines that are 4-5 feet (1.2-1.5 m) apart. Ask students to stand with their backs to each other.

Step 4: Have the leader stand to the side of the playing field.

Step 5: The leader must yell "cheetah" or "cheetal." The team called by the leader has to turn around and try to catch members of the other team who will be running to the base line that is in front of them. Players who are tagged are out of the game.

The winning team is the one that tags all of the members of the other team.

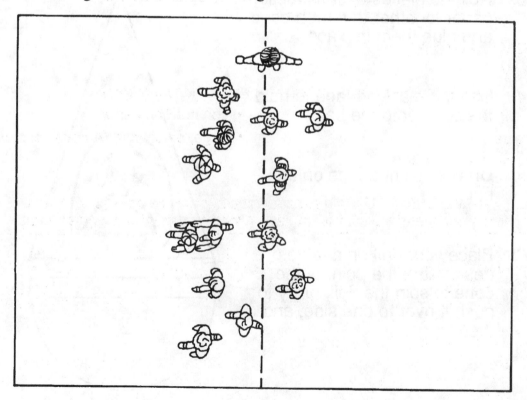

Native American Stick Dice and Pebble Game

In this activity, you will learn how to make and play two games that many Native American children enjoy.

Stick Dice
Materials:

- 3 craft sticks
- tempera paint (red, yellow, and black)
- paintbrushes

Directions:

Step 1: Paint one side of each craft stick red. Allow the paint to dry. Paint the other side of each craft stick yellow. Allow the paint to dry.

Step 2: Turn over one craft stick so that the red side is showing. Use black paint to draw a snake on it.

Step 3: Now play the game with one or more friends. Take turns throwing the three craft sticks. Add up the score, using the following chart.

3 red sides	3 points
3 yellow sides	2 points
2 red sides, 1 yellow side	1 point
2 yellow sides, 1 red side	0 points
snake	2 bonus points

The first person to earn 20 points is the winner.

Pebble Game
Materials:

- 15 small, smooth stones or pebbles
- scissors
- glue
- crayons or markers
- permanent marker
- construction paper
- large, empty can (A coffee can works well.)

Directions:

Step 1: Clean the stones. Use a permanent marker to write an X on five stones, an O on five stones, and a Z on five stones. Allow the permanent marker to dry.

Step 2: Cover the can with construction paper and glue. Then use crayons or markers to decorate the can.

Step 3: Put the stones into the can.

Step 4: Play the game with two or three other students. Have the players take a stone out of the can until it is empty. The winner is the person who has the most stones with the same letter.

A Jewish Dreidel

A dreidel is a type of top that Jewish children play with when they celebrate Hanukkah. Follow the directions to learn how to play the game.

Materials:

- dreidel pattern
- glue
- cup
- tokens
- pencil

Directions:

Step 1: Cut out the dreidel pattern shown below.

Step 2: Fold and glue the pattern into the shape of a cube.

Step 3: Gently push a sharpened pencil through the top and bottom of the cube.

Step 4: Give each player the same number of tokens. Have each player start the game by putting two tokens into the cup.

Step 5: Players spin the top and can win or lose the tokens that are in the cup.

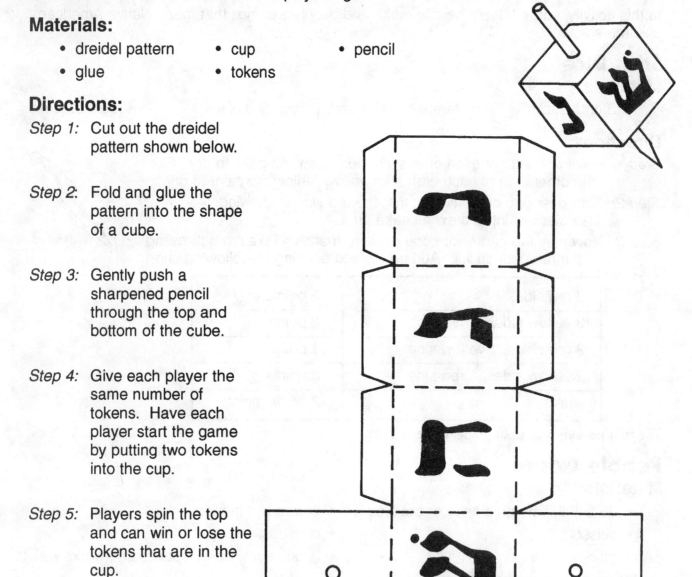

Use the following chart to play.

נ	Nun	You win nothing.
ג	Gimel	You win all of the tokens in the cup.
ה	He	You take half the tokens in the cup.
ש	Shin	You must put one more token in the cup.

Your Favorite Game or Toy

Directions: Draw a picture of your favorite toy or game. Then write a paragraph to tell why it is your favorite.

Bulletin Board Idea

Use the following bulletin board idea to introduce the section on music. The patterns shown below make the bulletin board quick and easy to create. Begin by covering the background with aluminum foil. Then use an opaque projector to enlarge and copy the patterns shown below. Make multiple copies of the musical note. Use the notes for the border of the bulletin board. Use construction paper to make labels for each of the instruments as shown. Finally, create the title "Everybody Listens to Music!" You may also wish to place a table in front of the bulletin board to create a learning/research center to help students find out more about music.

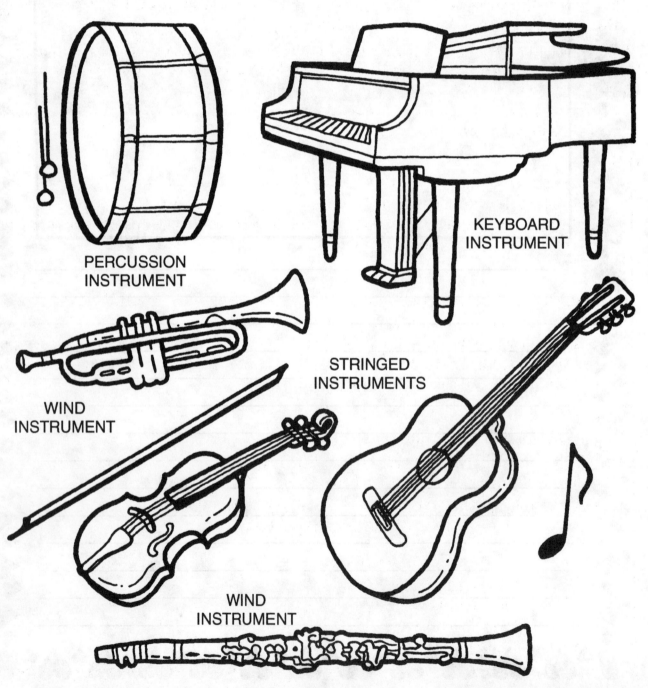

Introduction

People living in Europe, South America, North America, and Australia share a musical heritage. Music in these Western countries consists of classical and popular music. Symphonies, operas, and ballets are types of classical music. A variety of music, musical movie productions, rock and roll, country music, jazz, and folk music, are part of popular music.

People living in China, Japan, India, countries in the Middle East, and Indonesia listen to the same type of music. The music in these Asian countries sounds much different from the music enjoyed by people living in Western countries. This music uses different scales, methods of composing, and instruments.

Africans who live south of the Sahara Desert use music during ceremonies, rituals, and festivals. This music is composed primarily of rhythms. Most of the time the rhythms are created by the beating of drums, the ringing of bells, or the clapping of hands.

Native Americans share a rich heritage of music that was used in ceremonies, rituals, and social activities. Drums and rattles were used to accompany the voices that were singing. In some groups of Native Americans, flutes were also used.

Sample Plans

Lesson 1
- Introduce the section on music.
- Display a variety of instruments.
- Share personal experiences taking lessons to learn how to play an instrument, sing, or dance.
- Display the music bulletin board (page 122).

Lesson 2
- Introduce the vocabulary for music, then do a vocabulary activity (page 124).
- Select activities from Curriculum Connections (page 125).
- Discuss the types of music that are liked best.
- Make a Spanish tambourine (page 126).
- Learn the steps to some folk dances (pages 127-128).

Lesson 3
- Do a vocabulary activity (page 124).
- Select activities from Curriculum Connections (page 125).
- Take a poll to see who is taking musical lessons.
- Create a rattle like those used by some Native Americans (page 129).
- Put together an African-American banjo (page 130).

Lesson 4
- Select activities from Curriculum Connections (page 125).
- Learn how to make an Italian violin (page 131).
- Make an Asian xylophone (page 132).
- Write a song (page 133).

Background Information

The following chart shows the different types of instruments.

Stringed Instruments		Wind Instruments		Percussion Instruments	Keyboard Instruments	Electronic Instruments
Plucked: Mandolin Guitar Harp Lute	Bowed: Violin Viola Cello Bass	Woodwinds: Oboe English Horn Clarinet Bass Clarinet Flute Piccolo Bassoon Soprano Saxophone Tenor Saxophone Baritone Saxophone	Brasses: Trumpet Bugle Trombone French Horn Sousaphone Baritone Horn Flugelhorn Gong	Kettle Drum Snare Drum Bass Drum Bongo Drums Vibraphone Cymbals Sleigh Bells Chimes	Piano Harpsichord Pipe Organ	Electric Guitar Electric Piano Electric Organ Synthesizer

Vocabulary

You may wish to introduce the following vocabulary words at the beginning of this section: orchestra, classical music (symphonies, operas, ballets), popular music (country music, folk music, jazz, rock and roll), instrument, composer.

Note: Use the chart shown above in Background Information if you wish to have students learn the names of the different musical instruments.

Vocabulary Activities

You can help your students learn and retain the above vocabulary by providing them with interesting vocabulary activities. Here are a few ideas to try.

- Prepare a spinner to play Spin-A-Word by drawing lines to divide it into four equal parts. Mark each part with one of the following point values: 10 points, 20 points, 30 points, 40 points. Divide the class into two teams. Play the game by having each student spin the spinner and define a vocabulary word that you provide. A correct answer is worth the point value shown on the spinner. Then the spinner goes to the other team. A wrong answer means the spinner goes to the other team without any points being scored. The team with the highest total score at the end of a period of time that you designate is the winner.

- Ask students to create crossword puzzles or word search puzzles using the vocabulary words. Then the puzzles can be duplicated so they can be shared with the entire class.

- Have students make word scrambles by writing each vocabulary word with the letters rearranged on a 4" x 2" (10 cm x 5 cm) piece of construction paper. On the back of each piece of paper, have students write the word as it is correctly spelled. Then divide the class into two teams. Have students compete to unscramble the words and give meanings for them. Award one point for each correct answer. The winning team is the one with the most points at the end of a period of time designated by you.

Curriculum Connections

You may wish to use one or all of the following activities to supplement your own ideas about ways to integrate the *Celebrate Our Similarities* theme into your curriculum.

Language Arts:

1. Ask students to be silent for one minute and listen for sounds they can hear in the classroom. After the minute is over, have students brainstorm a list of all the sounds that they heard. Take the class outside. Repeat the activity by having students listen for one minute and then brainstorm a list of sounds they heard outside. Have students compare and contrast the sounds they heard inside the classroom with those that they heard outside.
2. Have students work as a class to write a school song.

Science:

1. Demonstrate for students how vibrations that make sound can be transferred from one solid object to another. Tape a tuning fork against a desk. Then gently touch the top of a glass with the tuning fork. Point out to students that the glass picks up the vibration from the tuning fork.
2. Have students fill several glasses that are the same size with different amounts of water. Have them tap a spoon against each glass to hear the differences in pitch and tone.

Social Studies:

1. Make a recording of different sounds. Examples include: a telephone ringing, a dog barking, a clock ticking, and a person sneezing. Ask students to listen to the recording and identify as many sounds as possible.
2. Take students to the school library. Have students work together in groups to research different musical instruments. Ask them to present a report to the class about the instruments.

Math:

Show students some sheet music. Point out that the meter is the fraction shown at the beginning of the music. Explain that the denominator, or bottom number of the fraction, identifies the type of note that gets one beat. The numerator, or top number of the fraction, tells how many beats are in a measure, or unit of time, for that piece of music.

Literature:

1. Divide the class into cooperative learning groups. Have students create skits from folk tales. See bibliography (pages 174-175) for suggestions of folk tales. Have students tape record sound effects for their stories. Then have the groups present their skits for the class.
2. Read aloud to students biographies of famous composers from around the world. Have students make a time line that shows when these famous composers lived.

Art:

Have students listen to classical music on cassette tapes, records, or compact discs. As students listen, ask them to draw the things the music makes them think of.

Life Skills:

1. Discuss careers in music—composer, songwriter, musician, performer, dancer, choreographer, choir director, band manager, teacher, and recording studio technician.
2. Invite an audiologist to speak to your class. Ask your guest to show students how hearing tests are given.

A Spanish Tambourine

In Spain, a tambourine is often used to keep the beat of a piece of music, a dance, or a song. In this activity, you will make a tambourine. Be sure to have an adult help you use a hammer safely.

Materials:

- aluminum pie plate
- 18 bottle caps
- hammer
- 2-3 yards (1.8-2.7 m) different colored ribbon
- 1 large nail
- ruler
- scissors

Directions:

Step 1: Carefully use the hammer and nail to make 18 holes close to the rim of the pie plate.

Step 2: Use the hammer and nail to make a hole in the center of each bottle cap.

Step 3: Cut 16 pieces of ribbon that are each 6 inches (15 cm) long.

Step 4: Tie the bottle caps to the pie plate, using the pieces of ribbon.

Step 5: Tie two long pieces of ribbon onto a hole in the pie plate. Then tie two more long pieces of ribbon onto a hole on the opposite side of the pie plate.

Step 6: Hold your tambourine with one hand and tap it against the palm of your other hand. Try playing your tambourine along with some music.

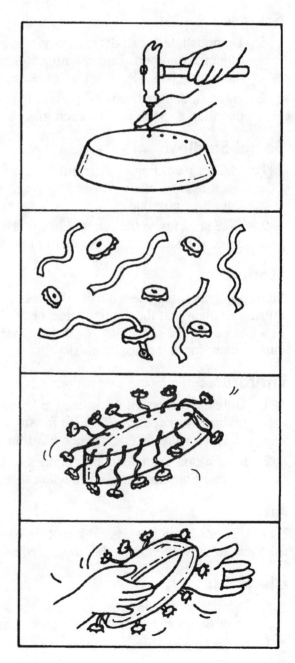

Folk Dancing

In this activity, students will discover that dancing is a popular activity throughout the world. Use this page and page 128 to introduce some simple folk dances to your students.

Israeli Horae

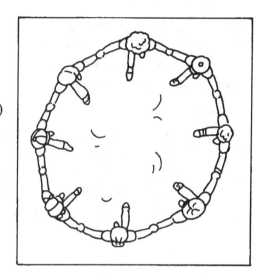

Directions:

Step 1: Have students hold hands in a circle. Tell them that they will be moving to the left. (You might want to check to be sure all students know which way is left.)

Step 2: Have students step to the side with their left feet.

Step 3: Have them cross their right feet behind their left feet.

Step 4: Have students step to the side with their left feet.

Step 5: Have them cross their right feet in front of their left feet.

Step 6: Have students repeat Steps 2-5.

American Bunny Hop

Use music that has a fast beat (4/4).

Directions:

Step 1: Have students form a single line, one behind the other, and hold each other's waists.

Step 2: Have them take four running steps, beginning with the right foot.

Step 3: Have students take hops on their left feet.

Step 4: Have them stamp their feet: right-left-right.

Step 5: Have students kick to their right sides.

Step 6: Have them kick to their left sides.

Step 7: Have students hop backwards three times.

Step 8: Have students repeat Steps 2-7.

Folk Dancing *(cont.)*

Here are some more simple folk dances your students will enjoy learning.

Latin American Rumba

Use lively Latin American folk music that has a fast beat (4/4). The directions below indicate which way the boys should move. The girls' movements should mirror the boys'. If students have difficulty coordinating their dance steps with a partner, have them try the dance by themselves.

Directions:

Step 1: Assign a partner for each student. If possible, have each girl paired with a boy. If this is not possible, assign one student to play the part of the girl and the other student to play the part of the boy.

Step 2: Have the partners stand facing each other. Have the boys step forward with their left feet and push their weight onto them.

Step 3: Have the boys step to the right with their right feet and push their weight onto them.

Step 4: Have the boys move their left feet close to their right feet. Have them push their weight onto their left feet.

Step 5: Have the boys step back with their right feet and push their weight onto them.

Step 6: Have the boys step to the left with their left feet and push their weight onto them.

Step 7: Have the boys move their right feet close to their left feet. Have them push their weight onto the right feet. Then have students repeat Steps 2–7.

Greek Hapapikos

Use fast Greek music.

Directions:

Step 1: Have students form a circle with their hands on one another's shoulders. Have them move their right feet one step to the right side.

Step 2: Have students cross their left feet over their right feet.

Step 3: Have them move their right feet one step to the right.

Step 4: Have students hop on their right feet.

Step 5: Have students move their left feet one step to the left.

Step 6: Have them hop on their left feet. Have students repeat Steps 2–7.

A Native American Rattle

The Native Americans who lived in the Eastern Woodlands enjoyed using music as part of their ceremonies. Rattles were often used to make the rhythm for the music. The rattles were made by filling turtle shells with pebbles or corn kernels. In this activity, you will make a rattle that looks like a turtle rattle.

Materials:

- Styrofoam box (such as those used for hamburgers)
- stick, about 1" (2.5 cm) in diameter and 8" (20 cm) in length
  markers
- popcorn kernels
- masking tape
- tempera paint or

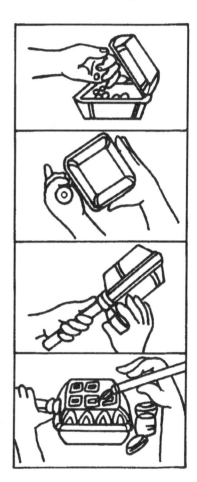

Directions:

Step 1: Place one handful of popcorn kernels into the Styrofoam box.

Step 2: Close the box. Then use masking tape to seal the box closed.

Step 3: Carefully push the stick into the front of the box.

Step 4: Use tape to keep the stick on the box.

Step 5: Make your box look like a turtle shell by using paint or markers.

Step 6: Create a rhythm with your rattle by shaking it.

An African-American Banjo

The banjo was first used in West Africa. African slaves brought this instrument with them to America.

Materials:

- round cardboard container
- scissors
- ruler
- six thumbtacks

- nylon fishing line
- paints
- glue

Directions:

Step 1:   Have your teacher help you cut a slit in each side of the container.

Step 2:   Take the top off the container. Put glue on the slits and push the ruler through them. Have the ruler stick out of the other end by about 1 inch (2.5 cm). Allow the glue to dry.

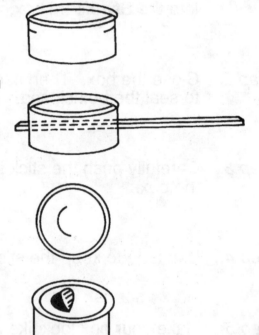

Step 3:   Have your teacher help you cut an arc in the top of the container as shown here. Pull the arc so that it bends up and make four small cuts in it.

Step 4:   Glue the top onto the container. Allow the glue to dry. Paint the top white. Allow the paint to dry.

Step 5:   Place two thumbtacks in the end of the ruler that is closest to the container.

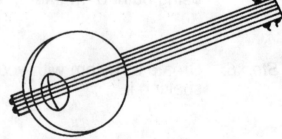

Step 6:   Place two thumbtacks on the sides of the ruler at the other end.

Step 7:   Tie the fishing line from the bottom thumbtack through the arc to the thumbtack on the side of the neck. Do the same with three more pieces of fishing line.

130

An Italian Violin

In Italy violin music is very popular. Musicians can be seen going from restaurant to restaurant as they play their violins. In this activity, you will make a violin.

Materials:
- empty tissue box
- 5 wide rubber bands
- one pencil, unsharpened

Directions:

Step 1: Place a rubber band on your pencil by stretching it from the eraser to the other end.

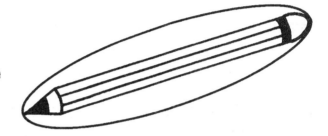

Step 2: Place four rubber bands on the tissue box over the opening. Be sure they are about 1/2 inch (1.25 cm) apart from one another.

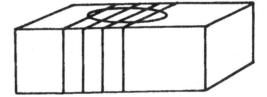

Step 3: Rub your bow (the pencil with the rubber band) across your violin (the tissue box with the rubber bands).

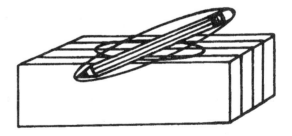

Step 4: Now try using rubber bands of different widths.

How do the widths of the rubber bands change the sounds they make?_____

An Asian Xylophone

The xylophone was first invented in Asia. Follow the directions shown below to make a xylophone.

Materials:

- eight fat pencils
- pencil sharpener
- scissors
- two skewers
- cardboard
- glue
- ruler
- two wooden beads

Directions:

Step 1: Sharpen each pencil to a different length, as shown here.

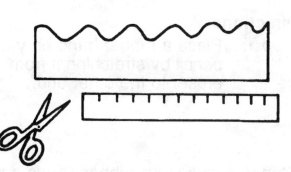

Step 2: Use a cardboard frame that looks like this. Use these measurements to make the frame.

    sides: 8.5" (21.25 cm) long

    long end: 6" (15 cm) long

    short end: 4.5" (11.25 cm) long

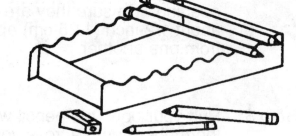

Step 3: Glue the pieces of the frame together.

Step 4: Place the pencils on the frame as shown here.

Step 5: Make a beater by gluing a wooden bead onto a skewer.

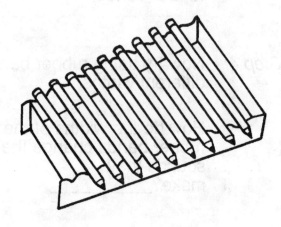

Step 6: Now play your xylophone.

Everybody Listens to Music!

A Song About You

Songs can be written for many reasons. They can be used to tell a story, point out a problem, or describe something or someone. In this activity, you will write a song that tells about you.

Directions:

Step 1: Use the box below to write eight things that are special about you.

1. _____
2. _____
3. _____
4. _____
5. _____
6. _____
7. _____
8. _____

Step 2: Pick a tune that you want to use for your song. What is the name of the tune you want to use?_____

Step 3: Use the box below to write words for your song, using the tune you chose. Be sure your song tells the special things you wrote in Step 1.

©1995 Teacher Created Materials, Inc.   133   #508 Celebrate Our Similarities

Bulletin Board Idea

Use the following bulletin board idea to introduce the section on arts and crafts. The patterns shown below make the bulletin board quick and easy to create. Begin by covering the background with butcher paper, aluminum foil, or tissue paper. Then use an opaque projector to enlarge and copy the patterns shown below. Paint the tip of the paintbrush with one color, and use different colored paints on the pallet to make the patterns look more like the real things. Allow the paint to dry. Place the paint pallet and paintbrush on the bulletin board. Around those patterns add a variety of different arts and crafts supplies, such as a ball of yarn, scraps of fabric, a pair of scissors, and a plastic small plastic bag with crayons in it. Finally, create the title "Arts & Crafts." You may also wish to place a table in front of the bulletin board to create a learning/research center to help students find out more about arts and crafts.

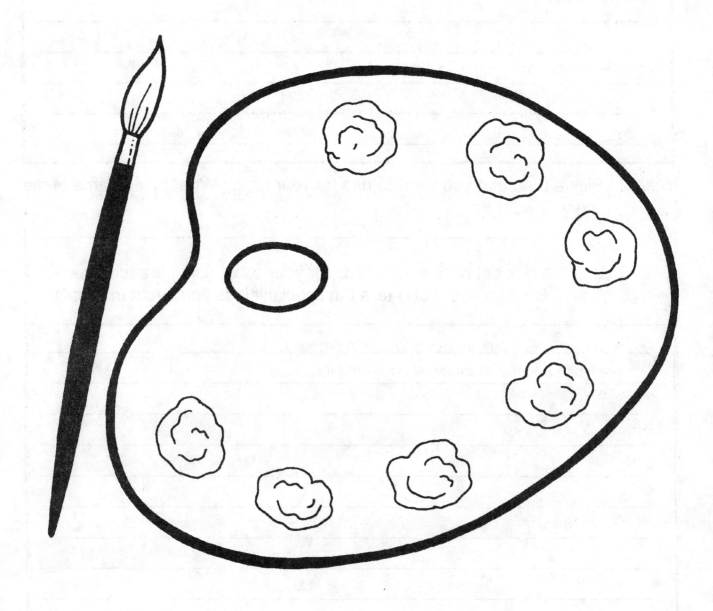

Introduction

People of all ages from all around the world enjoy doing arts and crafts. In this section, students will learn new art skills, increase their understanding of design, and improve their eye-hand coordination while recognizing and appreciating the contributions of different cultures. These activities provide students with the opportunity to be creative and make some things that they can share with others. The things they make can have an aesthetic value, a practical value, or both.

In recent years, arts and crafts activities have become an important part of classroom instruction. These types of tasks allow students to be active learners. Students learn how to follow steps in a process, an essential part of learning how to follow directions. At the end of each activity, students will have made a project that can be displayed for everyone to enjoy.

Sample Plans

Lesson 1

- Introduce the section on arts and crafts.
- Brainstorm a list of arts and crafts activities.
- Discuss the aesthetic and practical values of arts and crafts.
- Look at different books that contain arts and crafts activities.
- Display the arts and crafts bulletin board (page 134).

Lesson 2

- Introduce the vocabulary for arts and crafts; then do a vocabulary activity (page 136).
- Select activities from Curriculum Connections (page 137).
- Design a picture by using Mexican yarn art (page 138).
- Make a model of a Native American totem pole (page 139).

Lesson 3

- Do a vocabulary activity (page 136).
- Select activities from Curriculum Connections (page 137).
- Learn how people in Australia weave (page 140).
- Make a French potpourri ball (page 141).

Lesson 4

- Select activities from Curriculum Connections (page 137).
- Use the Cuna Indian method of making pictures (page 142).
- Make an African batik project (page 143).
- Write directions for an arts and crafts project (page 144).

Everybody Creates with Arts and Crafts!

Background Information

Arts and crafts are made by people all over the world. A wide variety of materials—wood, paper, clay, fabric, metal, beads, glass, reeds, yarn, and shells—are used to make these objects. These projects include such skills as painting, weaving, metalworking, carpentry, and stitchery. No matter what materials are used or what products are made, most arts and crafts involve people using their hands.

Early humans probably made crafts that were things they needed. To make these objects, they sharpened the edges of stones and then used those tools to cut pieces of wood. Picture writing was an art form that allowed these people to communicate ideas to one another. Later in history, people continued using their hands and hand tools to make things that served practical purposes, such things as clothing, baskets, and pottery. However, they also began using arts and crafts as a way to express religious beliefs.

During the Industrial Revolution arts and crafts became less important in supporting the needs of daily life. Advancements in technology meant that machines could make many goods that had previously been made by hand. These goods were produced at a faster rate and were less expensive.

Today, people of all ages enjoy making arts and crafts. Most of these people consider this work a hobby. However, some people earn a living at this, while still others use this creative outlet as therapy for physical or emotional problems.

Vocabulary

You may wish to introduce the following vocabulary words at the beginning of this section: supplies, materials, arts, crafts, hobby, tools, craft worker, artist, create, design, activity, project, product.

Vocabulary Activities

You can help your students learn and retain the above vocabulary by providing them with interesting vocabulary activities. Here are a few ideas to try.

- Divide the class into groups. Have each group be responsible for creating a game using the vocabulary words. Examples: Bingo, Wheel of Fortune, Jeopardy, Concentration, Spelling Bee. Have the class play the games the groups have created.
- Using a newspaper, have students cut out the letters to form the words from the list. See how many words students can make in 20 minutes. Have them make a class collage of the words they glue together.
- Have students do research to learn about a famous artist or craft worker. Ask them to write a short report about that person and use as many of the vocabulary words as possible.
- Before students enter the classroom, write several vocabulary words on the chalkboard as words of the day. As a warm-up activity, have students use a dictionary to locate the meanings of these words. Tell students to write the words and their meanings on notebook paper.

136 ©1995 Teacher Created Materials, Inc.

Curriculum Connections

You may wish to use one or all of the following activities to supplement your own ideas about ways to integrate the *Celebrate Our Similarities* theme into your curriculum.

Language Arts:

1. Display a variety of arts and crafts projects. Ask students to give a description, orally or in writing, of one of the projects.
2. Have students brainstorm a list of things that can be made using arts and crafts activities. Examples: paintings, sculptures, carvings, pottery, decorations, clothing, baskets, toys.
3. Have students create a list of safety rules to use when they are working on arts and crafts activities. Example: Do not run with scissors in your hand.

Science:

1. Explain to students that some craft workers use wood to make their projects. Have students name types of trees that could be used by these craft workers. If possible show students a piece of wood that shows the rings. Point out that a tree's age is determined by the number of rings it has. Explain that the rings can also indicate times of drought or plentiful rainfall.
2. Help students make their own plant dyes. Cherries, beetroot, and red cabbage can be used to make red dye. Onion skins can be used to make yellow dye. Spinach can be used to make green dye. Place a little water with the leaves or fruit in a pot. Bring the liquid to a boil, simmer for 15 minutes, then allow it to cool. Pour the liquid through a strainer or filter into a bowl. Then use a clean piece of white cloth to test the dye.

Social Studies:

1. As students learn about other countries, ask them to find examples of arts and crafts made by the people who live there.
2. Invite a local craftworker or artist to speak to the class. Have your guest bring some tools used in his or her occupation.

Math:

1. Provide story problems for students to solve that are related to arts and crafts and that involve linear measurement or weight.
2. Display pictures of different arts and crafts projects. Have students locate and identify geometric shapes, triangles, squares, rectangles, and circles, in these pictures.

Literature:

Select a book that includes arts and crafts activities. See the bibliography (page 174) for suggestions. Pick one activity and have students work together to make a flow chart that shows the steps needed to complete the project.

Music:

Use a record, cassette, or CD player to give students the opportunity to listen to folk music. Have students create a drawing or painting to illustrate one of the folk songs. Display the pictures in the school library.

Life Skills:

Arrange to take a field trip to a museum. After students return to school, ask them to discuss the exhibits they saw. Have them tell which exhibits they liked best and which ones they liked least.

Mexican Yarn Art

In this activity, you will learn how to make a picture with yarn. This type of art is very popular in Mexico.

Materials:

- cardboard square, 4" x 4" (10 cm x 10 cm)
- thick yarn, two colors
- glue
- scissors

Directions:

Step 1: Use the box shown here to draw a simple picture. You might wish to draw a heart, a flower, or a butterfly.

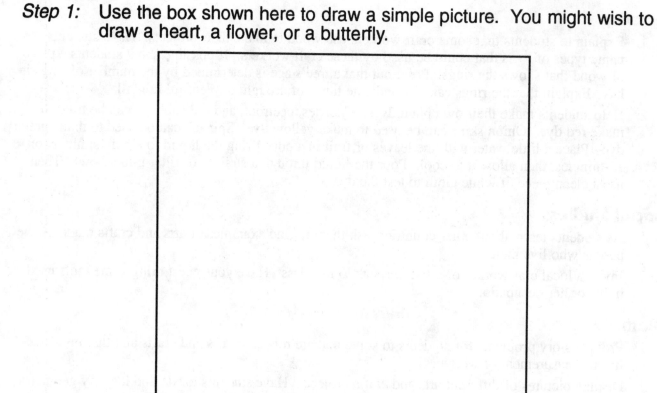

Step 2: After you have finished your picture, cut out the box and glue it onto the cardboard. Allow the glue to dry.

Step 3: Decide which color of yarn will be for the background and which will be for the picture you drew. Cut several pieces, each 12" (30 cm) long, of both colors of yarn.

Step 4: Rub glue over part of your picture. Zig-zag a piece of yarn onto the glue. Add more glue and yarn until the picture is complete. If your fingers get too sticky, wash your hands. Then do the same thing for the background.

A Native American Totem Pole

Native Americans who lived in the Pacific Northwest carved totem poles to tell about themselves. Use the totem pole pattern shown below to tell about yourself.

Directions:

Step 1: Think about how you are like three different animals. In each box of the pattern, draw an animal and write a sentence that tells how you are like that animal.

Example:

I am clever like a fox.

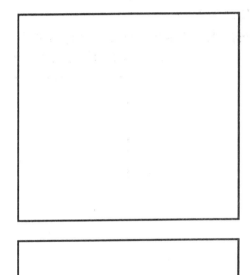

Step 2: Now cut out the pattern and glue the edges together to make a tube.

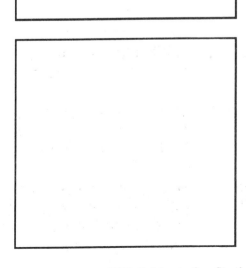

Australian Weaving

In Australia, many people raise sheep. They use the wool from the sheep to make yarn. Then the yarn is woven into many things, including clothing and blankets.

Use the directions shown below to make a bookmark out of yarn.

Materials:

- stiff cardboard, 8" x 2.5" (20 cm x 6.25 cm)
- scissors
- yarn
- needle with a blunt end

Directions:

Step 1: In each end of the cardboard, cut seven slits that are 1/2" (1.25 cm) long.

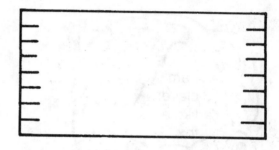

Step 2: Wrap the yarn around the cardboard from end to end seven times. Be sure to place the yarn in each slit as you go. After you have put the yarn into all of the slits, leave a long tail and then cut.

Step 3: Knot both ends of the yarn.

Step 4: Carefully thread the needle with a piece of yarn.

Step 5: Use the needle and yarn to weave across the yarn on the cardboard. Be sure to go over one thread and under the next. Each time you go back the other way, make sure you go in the opposite order. Be sure you do not make the weaving too tight by pulling too hard.

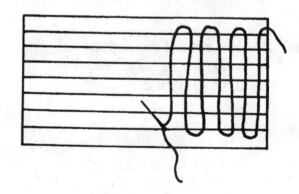

Step 6: Weave back and forth until the bookmark is completely done.

French Potpourri Balls

Potpourri is a French word that means "a mixture of things." It is used to refer to dried flower petals and spices that are mixed together to make a delicious scent. In this activity you will make a potpourri ball to keep in your dresser drawer or closet.

Materials:

- flower petals
- box
- spices (such as cinnamon, cloves, vanilla extract, peppermint extract)
- netted material
- ribbon
- scissors

Directions:

Step 1: Collect some sweet smelling flowers. Be sure to ask permission before you cut any flowers.

Step 2: Gently pull the petals off the flowers and place them into a box.

Step 3: Close the box and put it in a closet. Leave the flower petals in the box until they are dry. This will take about ten days.

Step 4: Cut a piece of netted material in the shape of a square. The larger the square is, the larger your potpourri ball will be.

Step 5: Place some dried flower petals in the middle of the netted square. Add some spices.

Step 6: Carefully pull up the sides and corners of the netted square. Tie a ribbon around the netted material just above the potpourri.

Cuna Indian Pictures

The Cuna Indians in Central America make special designs with cut-out pictures. In this activity, you will learn how to use paper to make a colorful cut-out picture.

Materials:

- construction paper, several colors
- paper clips
- scissors
- glue
- crayons or markers

Directions:

Step 1: Draw a simple design on a piece of construction paper, leaving about a 1" (2.5 cm) border all the way around. Some ideas for the picture include a flower, a fish, or a shell.

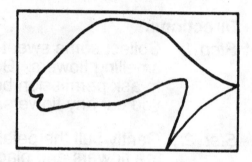

Step 2: Use your scissors to carefully cut out the pieces of your picture that are on the inside. You will still have the outline of your picture after those pieces are cut out.

Step 3: Place the outline of your picture on a second piece of construction paper that is a different color. Trace the inside pieces of the picture, but leave 1/4" (0.6 cm) border around the edge of each piece.

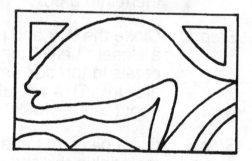

Step 4: Glue the outline of your picture onto a third piece of construction paper that is a different color.

Step 5: Glue the inside pieces in place. Allow the glue to dry.

Step 6: You may wish to add more layers, using different colors of construction paper.

142

African Batik

In West Africa, many people enjoy wearing clothes that are decorated using an art form called batik. In this activity, you will batik a handkerchief.

Materials:

- cotton handkerchief, white
- newspaper
- iron
- dye
- plastic tub
- wax blocks that have been melted
- paintbrushes

Directions:

Step 1: Use a pencil to draw any type of design on the handkerchief.

Step 2: Use the paintbrush to cover the design with melted wax. Anything that is not part of the design should not be covered with wax. Those areas will be dyed.

Step 3: Allow the wax to dry a little. Then pour cold water over it.

Step 4: Place the dye in a plastic tub. Place the handkerchief in the tub of dye. Allow the handkerchief to soak until the color looks very dark.

Step 5: Carefully take the handkerchief out of the tub. Pour cold water over it. Allow the water to rinse away any extra dye.

Step 6: Place the handkerchief on a flat surface to dry. After it has completely dried, put it between two pieces of newspaper.

Step 7: Ask an adult to iron the handkerchief between the pieces of newspaper, using a medium setting. This will remove the wax.

Writing Directions for an Arts and Crafts Project

Directions: Think of an arts and crafts project that you like to do. Use the boxes below to tell how to do that project. Add more boxes to the back of this page if you need them. Then draw a picture of what the project will look like when it is done.

Materials:

Step 1:

Step 2:

Step 3:

Step 4:

Step 5:

Step 6:

Step 7:

Step 8:

Bulletin Board Idea

Use the following bulletin board idea to introduce the section on celebrations. The pattern shown below makes the bulletin board quick and easy to create. Begin by gluing glitter onto some colorful wrapping paper so that it looks like fireworks. Use that paper to cover the background of the bulletin board. Place ribbon around the edges to make a border. Then use an opaque projector to enlarge and copy the pattern shown below. Add streamers, balloons, party hats, etc., to the bulletin board. Finally, create the title "Everybody Celebrates Special Days." You may also wish to place a table in front of the bulletin board to create a learning/research center to help students find out more about celebrations.

Introduction

People all over the world like to celebrate. Some celebrations are unique to a particular culture. Cultural celebrations reflect people's religious and political beliefs, as well as their values and traditions. Other celebrations are universal. This means that everywhere around the world people take the time to celebrate this special day. An example of this is New Year's Day. Each country's New Year's celebration may be organized differently, and it may occur at a different time. However, most people view the beginning of the new year as an occasion to celebrate.

In this section, students will learn to appreciate all different kinds of celebrations. They will see that people from around the world have days that are special to them. The ways in which people celebrate these special days can be very simple, or they can be extremely elaborate. Students will recognize that some celebrations are considered private affairs because they include only family members or the family and close friends, while other celebrations are considered very public because they involve large groups of people.

Sample Plans

Lesson 1

- Introduce the section on celebrations. Brainstorm a list of celebrations that are familiar.
- Display the bulletin board for celebrations (page 145)
- Bring photographs from home that show participation in different celebrations.
- Begin recording celebrations from around the world on a monthly calendar (page 157).

Lesson 2

- Introduce the vocabulary for celebrations; then do a vocabulary activity (page 147).
- Select activities from Curriculum Connections (page 148).
- Connect the celebrations theme to literature by reading *Happy New Year* (page 149).
- Select activities for *Happy New Year* (page 149).

Lesson 3

- Do a vocabulary activity (page 147).
- Select activities from Curriculum Connections (page 148).
- Tie straws together to make a Scandinavian star (page 150).
- Make a Mexican piñata, and then have students try and break it (page 151).

Lesson 4

- Select activities from Curriculum Connections (page 148).
- Use paper to make Russian Matreshka dolls (page 152).
- Create a Chinese dragon costume (page 153).

Lesson 5

- Select activities from Curriculum Connections (page 148).
- Make and fly a Japanese kite (page 154).
- Decorate a Jewish menorah (page 155).
- Color Easter eggs like Polish people do (page 156).
- Draw a favorite holiday and tell why it is a favorite (page 158).

Background Information

Celebrations are generally broken down into five groups: cultural, religious, political, heroic, and personal. Some celebrations fit into more than one category, and others started out as one type of celebration and have changed to another type because of changes in conditions and the passage of time.

Here are some examples of each type of celebration. Some of these may fit into more than one category.

Cultural: Kwanzaa, Grandparents' Day, Chinese Mid-Autumn Festival, Vietnamese Autumn Moon Festival, Halloween, Days of the Dead, Juneteenth

Religious: Passover, Easter, Hanukkah, Eid al-Adha, Christmas, Nirvana Day, Buddha's Birthday, Rosh Hashana

Political: Labor Day, Bastille Day, Hiroshima Day, Independence Day, Mexican Independence Day, United Nations Day, Memorial Day

Heroic: Washington's Birthday, Columbus Day, Martin Luther King, Jr. Day, Lincoln's Birthday

Personal: birthdays, anniversaries, graduations

Vocabulary

You may wish to introduce the following vocabulary words at the beginning of this section: celebration, festival, holiday, party, calendar, tradition, decorations, religious holiday, political holiday, heroic holidays, international holidays, personal holidays.

Vocabulary Activities

You can help your students learn and retain the above vocabulary by providing them with interesting vocabulary activities. Here are a few ideas to try.

- Divide the class into cooperative learning groups. Then have students work together to create an Illustrated Dictionary for the vocabulary words.

- Have students use the vocabulary words to write sentences, stories, or poems.

- Have students create a Celebrations Handbook. Ask them to use their vocabulary words as they describe different celebrations from around the world.

- Play Celebration Concentration. The goal of this game is to match vocabulary words with their definitions. Divide the class into groups of 2-5 students. Have students make two sets of cards the same size and color. On one set, have them write the vocabulary words. On the second set, have them write the definitions. All cards are mixed together and placed face down on a table. A player picks two cards. If the pair matches the word with its definition, the player keeps the cards and takes another turn. If the cards don't match, they are returned to their places face down on the table and another player takes a turn. Players must concentrate to remember the locations of the words and their definitions. The game continues until all matches have been made.

Curriculum Connections

You may wish to use one or all of the following activities to supplement your own ideas about ways to integrate the *Celebrate Our Similarities* theme into your curriculum.

Language Arts:

1. Invite students to tell about special celebrations that their families have. If possible, have students bring celebration photographs to show the class.
2. Have students write historical fiction stories about a family celebrating a special day. Allow time for students to share their stories with the class.
3. Ask students to make booklets that tell all about one holiday. Have them write about different aspects of the holidays and draw illustrations to go with their texts.
4. Write a list of celebrations on the chalkboard. Have students arrange and write the list in alphabetical order.

Social Studies:

1. Have students brainstorm a list of celebrations they know. Write the list on the chalkboard. Have students work in cooperative learning groups to research different celebrations.
2. Have a parade to celebrate some of the special days students are learning about. Have students march in the parade into other classrooms.
3. Have students discuss the importance of studying celebrations from around the world. Lead students to the conclusion that understanding and appreciating other cultures is the key to world peace.
4. Divide the class into cooperative learning groups. Have students work together to make a time line of celebrations.

Math:

1. Have students prepare a variety of recipes that are associated with different celebrations from around the world. Point out the different measurements used in each of the recipes.
2. Have students make up simple word problems that are related to celebrations. Example: On Tuesday, Marta bought seven balloons for her birthday party. On Wednesday, Tony gave her four more balloons for the big day. How many balloons did Marta have to blow up for her birthday party? (11)

Literature:

Allow students to have time in the school library. Have them locate books that tell about different celebrations.

Art:

Have students paint a mural showing celebrations taking place around the world. Hang the mural in the school cafeteria.

Physical Education:

Have students learn to do folk dances that are used during special celebrations. See bibliography (pages 174-175) for suggestions.

Life Skills:

Have students work in cooperative learning groups to plan a particular celebration. Have them make invitations, decorations, and plan the activities. If possible, allow the class to have the celebration. After the event, discuss what things went well and what they might do to improve it next time.

148

Literature Connection

> **Title:** *Happy New Year*
> **Author:** Emily Kelley
> **Publisher:** Carolrhoda Books (1984)

Summary: This is a colorful and informative book. It describes New Year's celebrations that take place all around the world. Maps that are provided in the book allow students to recognize the locations of the celebrations. Students will learn that New Year's Day is not always celebrated on the first of January. New Year's celebrations take place on a number of different days. The book also includes a helpful glossary.

Suggested Activities:

1. Read the book aloud to students. Then display a wall map of the world and provide copies of the world map (page 173) for students to color. Use the wall map to help students locate each of the countries mentioned in the book. Then have them color those countries on their map.

2. Ask students to discuss how they celebrate New Year's Day.

3. Learn how to say "Happy New Year" in different languages. Examples: Bonne Année (French), Gott Nytt Ar (Swedish), Hauoli Makahiki Hou (Hawaiian), Ein glückliches Neues Jahr (German), Szczesliwego Nowego Roku (Polish), An Nou Fericit (Romanian), Feliz Año Nuevo (Spanish), Onnellista Uuta Vuotta (Finnish).

4. Divide the class into cooperative learning groups. Ask students to brainstorm a list of reasons why they think New Year's Day is an important holiday for so many people around the world.

5. Ask students to pretend that they can travel to five different countries to learn more about their New Year's celebrations. First, have them pick five countries and use the book or reference materials to find out when people living in those countries have their New Year's celebrations. Remind students that they cannot be in two places at the same time. Then have students make a travel log that shows where and when they will go.

6. Divide the class into cooperative learning groups. Ask students to plan a New Year's celebration according to the traditions of a particular culture. Have them design the invitations, plan the activities, and make decorations. If possible, allow students to have the celebration on the appropriate date.

7. Write the words "Happy New Year" on the chalkboard. Ask students to use the letters to make up new words. Examples: nap, ear, we, pan, ray, raw, war, rap, pear, peer, harp, yarn.

8. Have students create a T-shirt design that could be worn to celebrate New Year's.

9. Have students paint a mural to show how people around the world celebrate New Year's.

10. Allow the class time in the school library. Have students do research to find out about the origin of New Year's.

11. Have students make up songs or poems about celebrating New Year's.

12. Have students write New Year's resolutions. Display the resolutions on a bulletin board.

Scandinavian Straw Star

In Sweden, straw ornaments are very popular during the Christmas season. Follow the directions shown below to make a straw ornament in the shape of a star.

Materials:
- five drinking straws
- red string
- scissors
- ruler

Directions:

Step 1: Use the red string to tie the ends of two straws together. Place the first two straws so they look like an upside down V.

Step 2: Tie a straw to the bottom of each straw in the upside down V. Place those two straws so they look like an X over the upside down V.

Step 3: Tie the two straws in the X where they cross over each other.

Step 4: Place the last straw over the top of the straws in the X.

Step 5: Tie the ends of the last straw to the tops of the straws in the X.

Step 6: Tie the straws together anywhere they overlap.

Step 7: Tie a piece of string with a loop onto the top of the star. Then hang up your straw star to decorate your classroom.

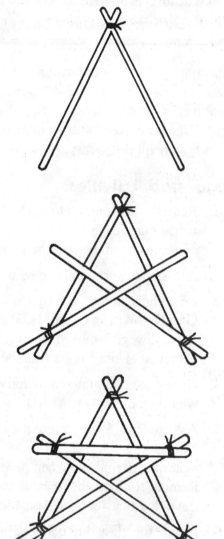

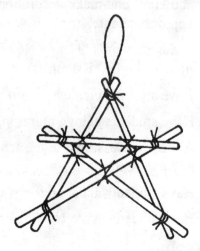

Mexican Piñata

Mexicans celebrate posadas for nine nights before Christmas. During this special celebration, the children break open a piñata. A piñata comes in many designs, such as a star, a donkey, or a bird. It is made from papier mâché covered with tissue paper and is filled with candy and toys. A piñata is hung up, and children take turns wearing a blindfold and swinging a stick to break it.

After it is broken, the candy and toys fall to the ground and the children grab as much as they can.

Materials:

- newspaper
- a 14" (35 cm) round balloon
- liquid starch used for laundry
- large bowl
- tissue paper
- construction paper
- yarn
- ruler
- scissors
- masking tape
- glue

Directions:

Step 1: Have students fold over a page of newspaper and roll it to make a 12" (30 cm) tube. Tell them to make four of these altogether. Explain that these will be legs for their piñata horse.

Step 2: Ask a volunteer to blow up the balloon. Tie a knot in the end of the balloon.

Step 3: Use the masking tape to attach the four tubes of newspaper to the balloon.

Step 4: Have a student fold over another page of newspaper and roll it to make a 6" (15 cm) tube. Use masking tape to attach this tube to the balloon. Tell students that this will be the neck.

Step 5: Ask a student to make the horse's head by forming a ball, using a piece of newspaper. Tape this ball to the top of the tube that is the neck.

Step 6: Have students cut strips of newspaper that are about 1" x 6" (2.5 cm x 15 cm). Pour the starch into a bowl. Have students put the strips of newspaper into the starch, remove excess starch by sliding them between two fingers, and apply them to the balloon. After the balloon is completely covered, allow it to dry.

Step 7: Have students add two more layers of newspaper strips, allowing it to dry between layers.

Step 8: Have them cut 2.5" (6.25 cm) strips of tissue paper. Fold the strips in half along the length. Show students how to make fringe by cutting slits along the folded edge. Turn the fold inside out, and glue the fringe onto the horse.

Step 9: Have students use construction paper to make the horse's mouth, eyes, and ears. Have them use the yarn to make a tail and mane. Glue these parts onto the horse. Allow the glue to dry.

Step 10: Carefully cut a flap in the horse's side. Put candy and small toys into the piñata. Glue the flap closed. After the glue has dried, hang up the piñata, and allow students to break it.

Russian Matreshka Dolls

Matreshka dolls are a popular gift during the Russian New Year. Matreshka dolls are made out of wood. They can look like little mothers, boys or girls growing up, or even members of a family. The dolls are different sizes so one can fit inside of the other.

In this activity, you will make some dolls that look like matreshka dolls.

Materials:
- matreshka doll patterns
- crayons or markers
- scissors
- tagboard
- glue
- stapler

Directions:

Step 1: Cut out the matreshka doll and apron patterns. Glue them onto tagboard, allow the glue to dry, and cut them out again.

Step 2: Place the aprons on the dolls. Staple along the edge of the sides and bottom of each apron to make a pouch.

Step 3: Color the dolls and their aprons. Put the dolls in the pouches from largest to smallest.

Chinese Dragon

In China, the Lantern Festival is part of their New Year's celebration. They have a parade which is led by a huge silk and bamboo dragon. In this activity, you will work with two or three other students to make a dragon costume.

Materials:

- white flat sheet for a twin-size bed
- sponges
- Styrofoam plates
- box, large enough to be worn over the head
- decorations, such as scraps of foil, streamers, and glitter
- red tempera paint
- construction paper
- scissors
- glue

Directions:

Step 1: Cut the sponges into shapes that look like a thumbnail.

Step 2: Place the sheet flat on the floor. Pour some tempera paint onto the Styrofoam plates. Dip the sponges into the paint and make scale prints on the sheet. Allow the paint to dry.

Step 3: Have an adult cut eyes and a zig-zag mouth out of the cardboard box. Paint the box red.

Step 4: After the glue dries, add decorations to the head—pieces of foil, streamers, and glitter.

Step 5: Use construction paper to make two cones for horns. Glue the horns to the top of the dragon's head.

Step 6: Glue one end of the sheet to the top back edge of the head. Allow the glue to dry.

Step 7: Pick one person to wear the box to be the dragon's head, and have the others stand under the sheet to be the body.

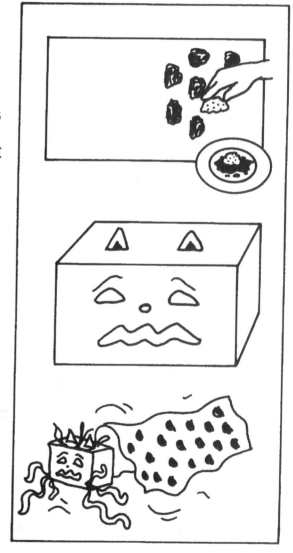

Japanese Kite

In Japan, kites are flown on May 5th for a celebration called Children's Day. The kites are shaped like a carp, which is a type of fish. The Japanese admire the carp because it must swim upstream. They believe this fish is strong and determined. In this activity you will make a kite that looks like a carp.

Materials:
- large paper grocery bag
- scissors
- three Styrofoam plates
- construction paper
- glue
- string
- stapler
- sponges
- orange, red, and yellow tempera paint
- streamers
- hole punch

Directions:

Step 1: Tuck in the corners on the closed end of the paper bag and staple.

Step 2: Cut a mouth for the carp out of the closed end of the bag.

Step 3: Pour each color of tempera paint onto a Styrofoam plate. Cut the sponges into three thumbnail shapes. Use the sponges and paint to make scales on both sides of the bag. Allow the paint to dry.

Step 4: Make two eyes from construction paper. Glue one eye on each side of the bag.

Step 5: Cut and glue long streamers onto the open end of the bag to make the tail. Allow the glue to dry.

Step 6: Use the hole punch to make a hole at the top and bottom of the mouth. Tie a short piece of string from one hole to the other. Then tie a long piece of string to the short one.

Take your kite outside on a windy day and try to fly it.

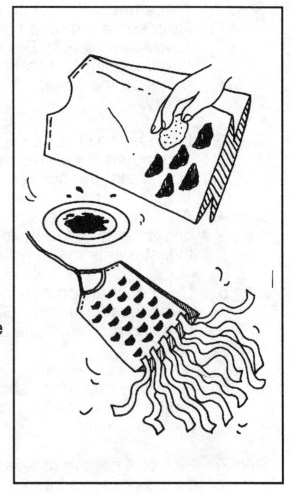

Jewish Menorah

Jewish families light candles on a menorah to celebrate Hanukkah.

Materials:

- aluminum foil
- scissors
- glue
- gold glitter
- crayons

Directions:

Step 1: Cut pieces of aluminum foil to cover the rectangles on the menorah.

Step 2: Glue the aluminum foil onto the menorah. Allow the glue to dry.

Step 3: Use crayons to color the candles.

Step 4: Then glue gold glitter for the candle flames.

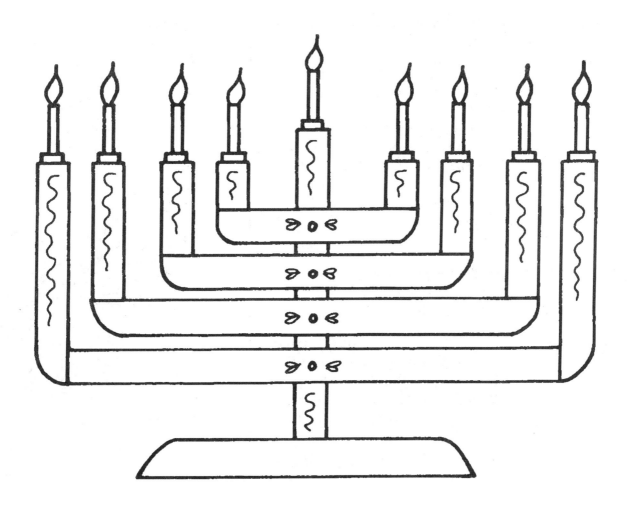

Polish Easter Eggs

Polish children enjoy painting eggs for Easter. Follow the directions shown below to learn how to paint eggs like children in Poland do.

Materials:

- raw egg
- bowl
- tempera paint
- ruler
- tape
- thin round skewer
- very narrow straw
- very narrow ribbon, 20" (50 cm) long
- scissors

Directions:

Step 1: Hold the egg over a bowl. Use the skewer to carefully make a tiny hole at the top and bottom of the egg. Try to break the yolk without breaking the shell.

Step 2: Remove the skewer. Gently blow through one hole so the inside of the egg comes out of the other hole. Be sure you are still holding the egg over the bowl! Gently rinse the egg with water and allow it to dry.

Step 3: Carefully put the narrow straw through the holes in the egg. Hold the egg by the straw and paint a design on it.

Step 4: After painting your design, place the straw on the edges of the bowl. The egg should be hanging over the bowl so it can dry without being touched.

Step 5: Fold the piece of ribbon in half. Tape the fold onto the bottom end of the straw.

Step 6: Carefully pull the straw along with the ribbon through the top of the egg. Undo the tape, leaving a loop of ribbon sticking out of the top hole and the two ends of ribbon sticking out of the bottom hole.

Step 7: Tie a bow with the two ends of the ribbon. Then hang the egg from the loop at the top.

A Monthly Calendar

Directions: Use this monthly calendar to write the names of special days that people celebrate.

Month: _____

Monday	Tuesday	Wednesday	Thursday	Friday	Saturday	Sunday

Everybody Celebrates Special Days!

Your Favorite Holiday

Many people have a favorite holiday. What is your favorite holiday to celebrate?

Directions: Draw a picture of yourself celebrating your favorite holiday. Then write a paragraph telling why it is your favorite holiday.

Bulletin Board Idea

Use the following bulletin board idea to introduce the section on friendship. The pattern shown below makes the bulletin board quick and easy to create. Begin by taking photographs of students or having them bring one from home. Cover the background of the bulletin board with butcher paper. Create a border of children's hands by having students trace one hand on construction paper and cutting it out or having students stick one hand in finger paint and placing their handprint on a piece of construction paper. Then use an opaque projector to enlarge and copy the pattern shown below. Place the hand pattern in the middle of the bulletin board. Hang the students' photographs around the hand pattern. Finally, create the title "Everybody Needs a Friend!" You may also wish to place a table in front of the bulletin board to create a reading center that has books about friendship. See the bibliography (page 174) for some suggested titles.

Introduction

In this section, students will learn that people from all around the world need and want friends. You may wish to begin this section by having students brainstorm a list of words that describe what a friend is. Make a word web with "A friend is..." in the center circle and the words that students suggest in the connecting circles.

Example Word Web

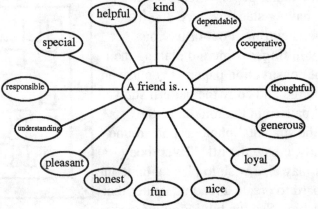

Sample Plans

Lesson 1

- Brainstorm and make a friendship word web (page 160).
- Display books that tell stories about friendships.
- Do a book report about a friendship story.
- Display the friendship bulletin board (page 159).

Lesson 2

- Introduce the vocabulary for friendship; then do a vocabulary activity (page 161).
- Select a Curriculum Connections activity (page 162).
- Role-play ways to keep and make friends.

Lesson 3

- Do a vocabulary activity (page 161).
- Select a Curriculum Connections activity (page 162).
- Make Samoan and Hawaiian leis (page 163).
- Give someone a handmade Mexican amigo bracelet (page 164).
- Interview a friend to find out more about that person.

Lesson 4

- Select a Curriculum Connections activity (page 162).
- Make a Native American friendship stick (page 165).
- Use students' names to make a friendship seek and find (page 166).
- Write a letter to a friend (page 167).

Background Information

The following ideas about friendship can be used in a discussion with students. You may wish to present these to students or lead them toward these conclusions.

- Everybody wants and needs friends.
- Sharing is an important part of friendship.
- The friends you choose should tell you a great deal about yourself.
- Be honest. Tell your feelings to your friends.
- If you want a friend, you need to be a friend.
- Real friends will respect you for who you are.
- Friendships can and do change as people get older or develop other interests.
- Find friends who share your interests.
- No one is perfect. Everyone has strengths and weaknesses.
- It is important to be a good listener.
- A friend is loyal in good and bad times.
- A friend is dependable and helpful.
- Friends are bound to argue at times. Remember that every argument has two sides.
- Learn how to apologize.
- If you need help dealing with friendships, do not hesitate to ask an adult, such as your parents, teacher, school counselor, scout leader, or athletic coach.

Vocabulary

You may wish to introduce the following vocabulary words at the beginning of this section: friend, friendship, pal, buddy, cooperation, sharing, compromise, helpful, honest, kind, dependable, thoughtful, generous, loyal, nice, pleasant, understanding, responsible, special.

Vocabulary Activities

You can help your students learn and retain the above vocabulary by providing them with interesting vocabulary activities. Here are a few ideas to try.

- Have students play Definition Relay. Divide the class into teams. Each member of a team must look up a vocabulary word and write down its definition, then pass the list on to another member of the same team. Allow students to continue working until the end of a time designated by you. At the end of the time limit, have the teams exchange word lists. Ask students to check each other's definitions. The team with the most correct definitions wins the relay. You can vary this game by calling time when all of the members of one team have written down a definition.

- Divide the class into cooperative learning groups. Then have students work together to create an Illustrated Dictionary for the vocabulary words.

- Before students enter the classroom, hide index cards around the room, some with vocabulary words written on them and others with definitions on them. When the class arrives, divide them into two teams to play Vocabulary Hide and Seek. Allow students to search the room for a period of time that you designate. Teams can score a point by matching a word with its definition. The winning team is the one with the most points at the end of the time period.

Everybody Needs a Friend!

Curriculum Connections

You may wish to use one or all of the following activities to supplement your own ideas about ways to integrate the *Celebrate Our Similarities* theme into your curriculum.

Language Arts:

1. Arrange for students to write to pen pals in another classroom at your school, another school in your community, or in another state.

2. Ask students to brainstorm a list of the characteristics that would make a person a good friend. Then have them write poems about friendship that describe some of these characteristics. Provide time for students to share their poems with the class.

3. Have students sit in a circle. Explain that this is a "friendship circle" and they will have the opportunity to say something nice about their classmates. Have each student make a positive statement about every other student in the class. After everyone has had a turn, ask students how they felt about the comments that were made.

Social Studies:

1. Have students brainstorm a list of ways to make and keep friends.

2. Explain to students that during colonial times, women used to make "friendship quilts" with their friends. Each square on the quilt would have someone's name embroidered on it. Cut large squares from white construction paper. Have students use crayons to write their names in a decorative way on a square. Then glue the squares onto a piece of butcher paper.

3. Have students learn how to say "friend" in different languages. Examples: "freund" in German, "mate" in Australian English, "tomodachi" in Japanese.

Science:

Have students write notes to friends, using "invisible ink." Have them make their invisible ink by squeezing lemon juice into a small bowl. Tell them to use paintbrushs and the lemon juice to write their notes. Allow the lemon juice to dry. Then ask students to give their notes to friends in the class. In a small jar, make a mixture of water with a little bit of iodine. Have students use the paintbrush and the iodine and water mixture to reveal the message that was written with the lemon juice.

Math:

Have students create word problems about friends doing activities together. For example, students might write a word problem about how much money two friends spend during an outing to a movie.

Literature:

1. Have students sit with partners and read books or stories together.

2. Read aloud a story about friendship. See the bibliography (pages 174-175) for suggestions. Then have students create a mural to show the major events in the story. Display the mural in the school library.

Art:

1. Provide students with a large safety pin and some colored beads. Have students open the pin and place a variety of beads on it to make a "friendship pin."

2. Use poster board to create a T-shirt pattern for students to use. Have students trace the T-shirt pattern onto butcher paper. Then have them write their names on the T-shirt and draw two pictures showing information about themselves that they would like a friend to know.

Samoan and Hawaiian Leis

Follow the directions below to learn how to make two different types of leis.

Samoan Candy Lei

Materials:

- hard candies in wrappers with twisted ends
- colored string
- scissors

Directions:

Step 1: Place the twisted ends of two pieces of candy over each other.

Step 2: Use a piece of string to tie the ends together.

Step 3: Connect a third piece of candy in the same way. Add more pieces of candy until the lei is long enough. Then give your lei to a friend.

Hawaiian Lei

Materials:

- crêpé paper
- scissors
- ruler
- needle
- thread

Note: Have an adult help you sew the lei.

Directions:

Step 1: Cut a piece of crêpé paper that is 2" (5 cm) wide and 2-3 yards (1.8-2.7 m) long. If you need more crêpé paper, you can cut another strip later.

Step 2: Cut a long piece of thread. Thread the needle. Then tie a knot at the end of the thread.

Step 3: Sew through the center of the crêpé paper, using a long running stitch.

Step 4: As you sew, twist and gather the crêpé paper toward the knot in the thread. This will make the paper look like flowers.

Step 5: At the end, sew over the last stitch several times and knot the thread. Tie the ends of the lei together.

Step 6: Place the lei over a friend's head.

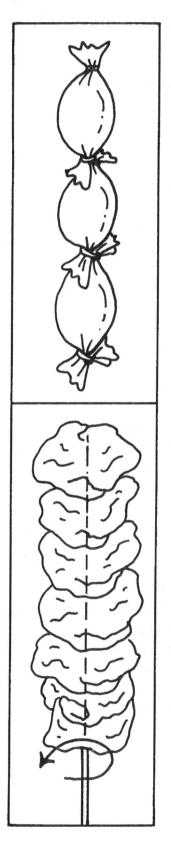

Everybody Needs a Friend!

Mexican Amigo Bracelet

In Mexico, amigo bracelets are a popular way to tell other people that you want to be their friend. The people who get an amigo bracelet wear it with pride. Someone who wears a large number of amigo bracelets probably has many friends. There are different ways to make an amigo bracelet. In this activity, you will learn one of them.

Materials:
- colored string
- ruler
- scissors
- tape

Directions:

Step 1: Cut three pieces of different colored string that are each about 20" (50 cm) long.

Step 2: Knot the pieces of string together at one end.

Step 3: Tape the knot to a flat surface, such as a desk or table.

Step 4: Begin braiding the three pieces of string. Do this by crossing the left string over the one in the center and then the right string over the one that is now in the center.

Step 5: Continue braiding until you are close to the ends of the strings. Then tie a knot with the loose ends. Remove the tape.

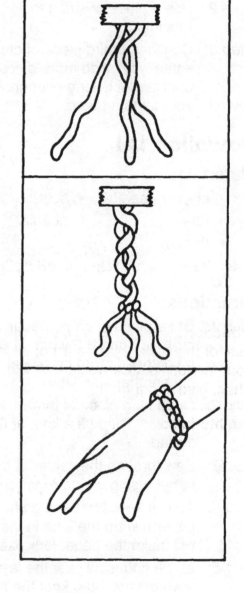

Step 6: Give your amigo bracelet to a friend. Place it on his or her wrist and tie a knot to join the two ends together.

Native American Friendship Stick

Some Native Americans who lived in the southwestern part of the United States gave friendship sticks to celebrate special occasions. The person who got a friendship stick felt very honored. Friendship sticks were made from carved branches that were 22" (55 cm) long. Some were painted to look like an animal, such as a snake or a lizard. Others had natural things, such as leaves, stones, feathers, or cones, attached to them. There were even some that were painted and had things added to them. Usually the bottom of the stick would be sharpened to a point. Then the stick could easily be pushed into the ground.

Here are some examples of friendship sticks.

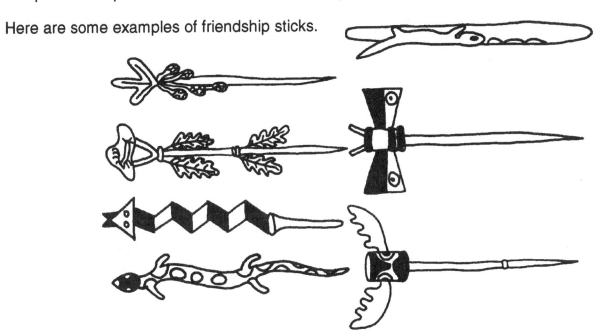

Directions: In this activity, you will design a friendship stick. Think about what you would use for the stick. Make a list of all the materials you would use. Then draw a picture of what your friendship stick would look like. If possible, make your stick with the materials you listed. Then, give it to a friend.

Materials:	My Friendship Stick:

Friendship Seek and Find

Directions:

Step 1: In the box below, make a list of the first names of all the students in your class.

Step 2: Then write the names below so that one letter is in each box. The names can go from side to side (◄►), up or down (↕), or across from corner to corner (↗ ↘).

Step 3: After you have used all of the names, fill in any extra boxes with any letter that you choose.

Step 4: Now trade papers with a friend and try to solve each other's seek and find.

Write a Letter to a Friend

In this activity, you will write a letter to a friend. Think about what you would like to tell one of your friends.

Here is an example of a friendly letter.

December 20, 1997

Dear Tomás,

I am so excited that you are coming to visit next weekend. We will be waiting for you at the airport when you arrive. I have some exciting things planned for us to do while you are here. I can hardly wait! I'll see you soon.

Your friend,

Julian

Directions: Now write a letter to one of your friends.

Date_____

Dear _____ ,

_____

_____

_____

_____

_____

_____

_____

_____ ,

_____

Multicultural Festival

Divide the class into cooperative learning groups and have a "Multicultural Festival." Have students brainstorm to make a list of activities they could use to tell other students about similarities among people or use the suggestions that are provided below. Then have students make the necessary preparations for the "Multicultural Festival." Finally, have students invite other classes to participate in this event.

Invitations: Using the form on page 169, have students make invitations to ask other classes to come to this special event. Have students make advertisements for the hallway that will make teachers and students want to attend.

Advertising: Have students create posters that advertise the Multicultural Festival. The advertisements should include important information and make the event look attractive.

Program and Decorations: Have students make a program that tells about the different events and displays that will be part of the celebration. Then ask students to decorate the room, using streamers, balloons, etc.

Big Books: Have students make big books that tell stories that come from different cultures. Punch three holes on the left-hand side of six pieces of poster board. Have students use one piece of poster board to create a cover for their big book. Then have them use the rest of the poster board to illustrate five events from the story and write a short summary of each event. Ask students to put the pieces of poster board in order according to the events in the story. After the pieces of poster board are in order, have students connect the pages with metal rings or yarn. Allow students to use their big books to retell their stories to younger children.

Postcards: Have students make postcards that show the following: different types of houses, clothes, transportation, and special holidays.

Folk Music and Folk Tales: Have students sing folk songs, perform folk dances, or role-play some folk tales.

Vehicles: Ask students to bring models of different types of transportation. If possible, have students set up an electric train set or use remote-controlled vehicles.

Guest Speakers: Invite people from the community to teach some basic vocabulary words in a foreign language.

Posters: Have students make posters to display around school that promote world peace and cooperation among the people of the world.

Heritage Quilts: Have students create heritage quilts (page 172) that tell about people from different cultures.

Recipes: Have students locate and make recipes from different cultures. Family members and local restaurants may be valuable resources for recipes. Try some of the recipes shown in this unit.

Learning Centers: Have students set up learning centers, using world themes that feature toys, money, and arts and crafts.

Student Guides: Ask individual students to act as guides during the celebration. Their jobs can be to show visitors around during the celebration activities.

Mural: Have students make a mural that shows some of the ways in which people are similar.

168

Invitation to a Multicultural Festival

Make copies of the following invitation. Have students correctly fill out the information that is needed. Then ask them to decorate the invitation.

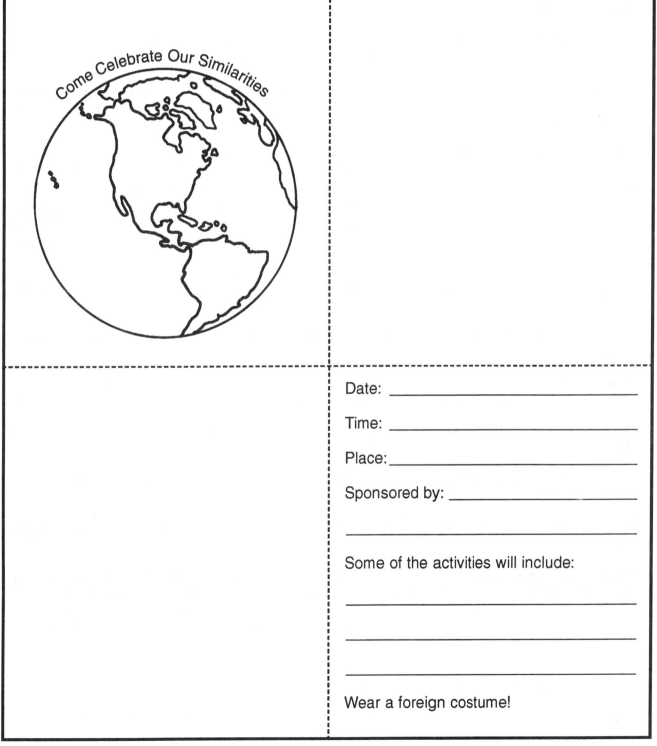

Come Celebrate Our Similarities

Date: _____

Time: _____

Place:_____

Sponsored by: _____

_____

Some of the activities will include:

_____

_____

_____

Wear a foreign costume!

People Books

Have students make books that tell about different countries and show how people from those countries dress. They can use information that they learned in this unit, or they can do research for this activity.

Materials:

- large piece of construction paper, 12" x 18" (20 cm x 45 cm)
- small piece of construction paper, 6" x 6" (15 cm x 15 cm)
- scraps of construction paper
- scissors
- glue
- crayons or markers

Directions:

Step 1: Have students fold the large piece of construction paper in half along the length. Then unfold it.

Step 2: Now have them fold the large piece of construction paper in half along the width. Have them fold it in half again. Then ask them to completely unfold it.

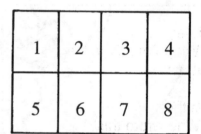

Step 3: Have students use a pencil and lightly number the rectangles from one through eight as shown here.

Step 4: Show students how to cut off rectangles five and eight, but do not allow them to throw those pieces away.

Step 5: Have students fold over rectangles one and four so that rectangles two and three are covered.

Step 6: To make arms, show students how to glue rectangles five and eight behind rectangles two and three as shown here.

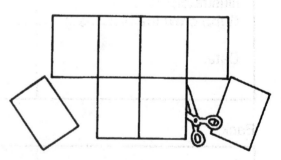

Step 7: Have students cut a circle from the square piece of construction paper and glue it to the body.

Step 8: Show students how to cut out a small triangle at the fold between rectangles six and seven. Have them erase all of the numbers on the rectangles.

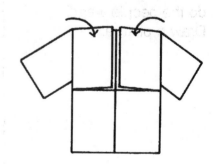

Step 9: Have students add scraps of construction paper to make hands and feet. They can also use the scraps to make clothes and hats.

Step 10: Have them use crayons or markers to draw faces, hair, and designs on the clothing. Then have them write the information behind the flaps under the head.

Travel Pamphlets

Make a travel pamphlet that tells about another country. Do research and use the information that you learned in this unit for your pamphlet.

Materials:

- white construction paper
- crayons or markers
- pencil

Directions:

Step 1: Plan what you will write and draw in the boxes shown below.

Step 2: Then fold a piece of white construction paper so that it opens like an accordion. (It should not open like a book.)

Step 3: Use your plan to make the final draft of your pamphlet.

Front:

Title: (What country is this about?) Author: (Who wrote this?) Illustrator: (Who drew the pictures?) Date:	Tell where this country is and draw a map.	Tell about the food the people in this country eat. Draw a picture.

Back:

What kind of clothes do the people wear? Draw a picture.	What kind of houses do the people have? Draw a picture.	Tell some other interesting things about that country. Draw some pictures.

Heritage Quilt

In this culminating activity, you will work with two or three other students to make a heritage quilt that shows how people from around the world are similar. Here are some things you might want to show on your quilt: houses, clothing, transportation, story characters and events, games and toys, arts and crafts, or celebrations.

Materials:
- one sheet of butcher paper, 2' x 2' (60 cm x 60 cm)
- 16 construction paper squares – each: 6" x 6" (15 cm x 15 cm)
- markers or crayons
- glue

Directions:
Step 1: Pick 16 objects or events that you want to show on your quilt. On each quilt square, you will draw a picture of one object or event and write a sentence to tell about it. Use the space below to plan your quilt.

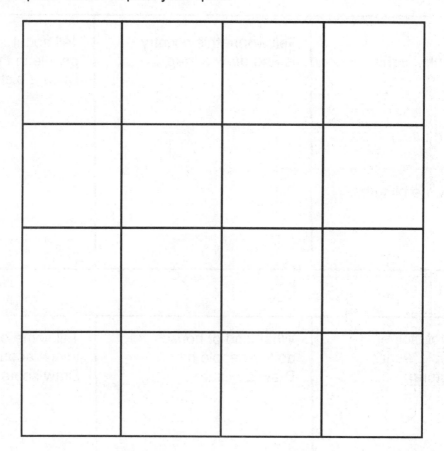

Step 2: Decorate each construction paper square by drawing a picture and writing a sentence about it.

Step 3: Lay your squares on the butcher paper according to the plan you made above. Glue the squares down onto the butcher paper. Allow the glue to dry.

Step 4: Display your heritage quilt on a wall or bulletin board.

World Map

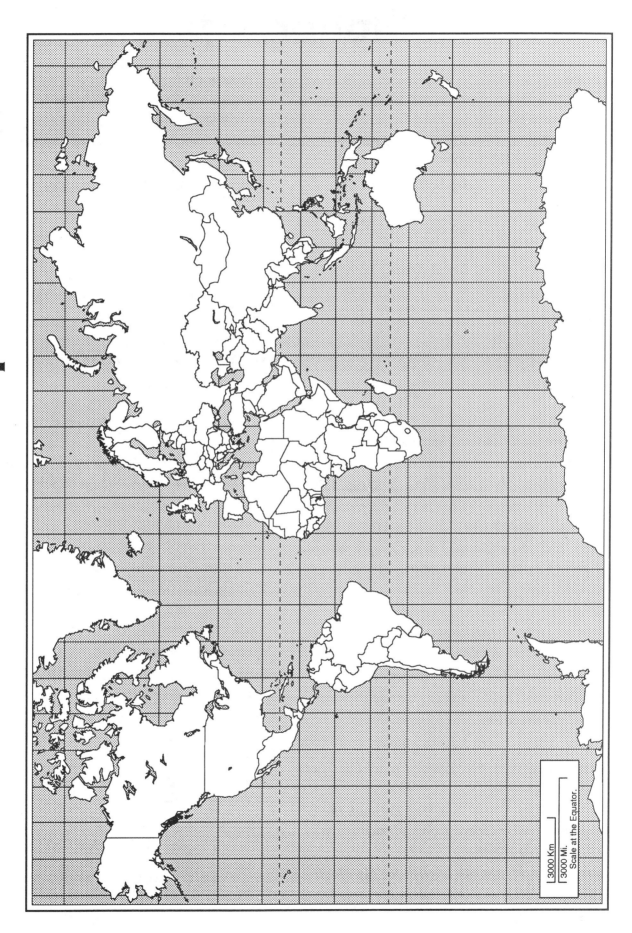

3000 Km
3000 Mi.
Scale at the Equator.

Bibliography

Food

Coronado, Rosa. *Cooking the Mexican Way.* Lerner, 1992.

Friedman, Ina. *How My Parents Learned to Eat.* Houghton Mifflin, 1984.

Kandoian, Ellen. *Is Anybody Up?* Putnam, 1989.

Modesitt, Jeanne. *Vegetable Soup.* Macmillan, 1988.

Morris, Ann. *Bread Bread Bread.* Lothrop, 1989.

Sproule, Anna. *Food for the World.* Facts on File, 1987.

Turner, Dorothy. *Bread.* Carolrhoda Books, 1988.

Turner, Dorothy. *Eggs.* Carolrhoda Books, 1989.

Clothing

Costumes and Clothes. Marshall Cavendish, 1989.

Morris, Ann. *Hats, Hats, Hats.* Lothrop, 1989.

Rohmer, Harriet, and Rosalma Zubizarreta. *Uncle Nacho's Hat.* Childrens Press, 1989.

Weil, Lisl. *New Clothes: What People Wore — from Cavemen to Astronauts.* Macmillan, 1988.

Shelter

Durros, Arthur. *This Is My House.* Scholastic, 1992.

Morris, Ann. *Houses and Homes.* Lothrop, 1989.

Communication

Agard, John. *The Calypso Alphabet.* Holt, 1989.

Farris, Katherine. *Let's Speak French!* and *Let's Speak Spanish!* Viking, 1993.

Haskins, Jim. *Count Your Way Through the Arab World.* (China, Japan, Mexico). Carolrhoda Books, 1987-1991.

Street, Muriel. *I Speak English for My Mom.* Albert Whitman, 1989.

Transportation

Baer, Edith. *This Is the Way We Go to School.* Scholastic, 1990.

Ganly, Helen. *Jyotis Journey.* Andrew Deutsch Ltd., 1986.

Milord, Susan. *Hands Around the World.* Williamson Publishing, 1992.

School

Baer, Edith. *This Is the Way We Go to School.* Scholastic, 1990.

Delacre, Lulu. *Time for School, Nathan!* Scholastic, 1989.

Stories

Goble, Paul. *Iktomi and the Buzzard.* Orchard, 1994.

Goode, Diane. *The Diane Goode Book of American Folk Tales & Songs.* Random, 1992.

Greene, Ellin. *The Legend of the Cranberry: A Paleo-Indian Tale.* Simon & Schuster, 1993.

Hadley, Tessa. *Legends of Earth, Air, Fire, and Water.* Cambridge University Press, 1988.

Jefferies, David. *Multicultural Folk Tales.* Teacher Created Materials, 1992.

Kipling, Rudyard. *Just So Stories.* Harper Collins, 1991.

Retan, Walter. *Favorite Tales from Many Lands.* Grosset & Dunlop, 1989.

Sierra, Judy, and Robert Kaminski. *Multicultural Folktales.* Onyx Press, 1991.

Swartz, Howard, and Barbara Ruch. *The Diamond Tree: Jewish Tales from Around the World.* Harper Collins, 1991.

Yalen, Jane. *Street Rhymes Around the World.* Wordsong, 1992.

Games & Toys

Bonners, Susan. *The Wooden Doll.* Lothrop, 1991.

Brigandi, Pat. *String Magic.* Scholastic, 1993.

Bibliography *(cont.)*

Grunfeld, Frederic V. *Games of the World.* UNICEF, 1982.

Lankford, Mary D. *Hopscotch Around the World.* Morrow, 1992.

Vecchione, G. *The World's Best Outdoor Games.* Sterling, 1992.

Zubroushi, Bernie. *Tops.* Morrow, 1989.

Music

DeCesare, Ruth, ed. *Songs of Hispanic Americans.* Alfred Publishing, 1991.

King, Sandra. *Shannon: An Ojibway Dancer.* Lerner, 1993.

Mattox, Cheryl Warren, ed. *Shake It to the One That You Love the Best: Play Songs and Lullabies from Black Musical Traditions.* Warren-Mattox Productions (3817 San Pablo Dam Road #336, El Sobrante, CA 94803), 1989.

Modesitt, Jeanne, comp. *Songs of Chanukah.* Little, 1992.

Smith, Lucy. *Dance.* Osborne Publishing Ltd., 1987.

Arts and Crafts

Cavanaugh, Betty Gaglio. *Multicultural Art Activities.* Teacher Created Materials, 1994.

Corwin, Judith Hoffman. *Asian Crafts.* Watts, 1992.

Corwin, Judith Hoffman. *Latin American and Caribbean Crafts.* Watts, 1992.

Celebrations

Ahsan, M.M. *Muslim Festivals.* Rourke Enterprises, Inc., 1987.

Ancona, George. *Powwow.* Harcourt Brace Jovanovich, 1993.

Churchill, E. Richard. *Holiday Paper Projects.* Sterling, 1992.

Corwin, Judith Hoffman. *Jewish Holiday Fun.* Julian Messner, 1987.

Dorros, Arthur. *Tonight Is Carnaval.* Dutton, 1991.

Everix, Nancy. *Ethnic Celebrations Around the World.* Good Apple, 1991.

Jasmine, Julia. *Multicultural Holidays.* Teacher Created Materials, 1994.

Kelley, Emily. *Christmas Around the World.* Childrens Press, 1986.

Kelley, Emily. *Happy New Year.* Carolrhoda, 1991.

Lowery, Linda. *Earth Day.* Carolrhoda, 1991.

Pennington, Daniel. *Itse Selu: Cherokee Harvest Festival.* Charlesbridge Publishing, 1994.

Silverthrone, Elizabeth. *Fiesta!: Mexico's Greatest Celebrations.* Millbrook, 1992.

Stevens, Beth D. *Celebrate Christmas Around the World.* Teacher Created Materials, 1994.

Van Straalen, Alice. *The Book of Holidays Around the World.* Dutton, 1986.

Friendship

Berry, Joy. *Every Kid's Guide to Making Friends.* Children's Press, 1987.

Hale, Janet. *Friendship.* Teacher Created Materials, 1991.

Macmillan, Diane and Dorothy Freeman. *My Best Friend Martha Rodriguez.* Messner, 1986.

Yingling, Phyllis S. *My Best Friend Elena Pappas.* Messner, 1986.

General Multicultural

Adoff, Arnold. *All the Colors of the Race.* Beech Tree Books, 1992.

Kane, Susan, David Cavanaugh, and Jane Gilbert. *Celebrating Diversity.* Teacher Created Materials, 1993.

Kerklen, Susan. *How My Family Lives in America.* Bradbury Press, 1992.

Schaff, Barbara, and Sue Roth. *A Trip Around the World.* Teacher Created Materials, 1993.

Sterling, Mary Ellen. *Peace.* Teacher Created Materials, 1992.

Answer Key

Page 15
1. butter
2. cheese
3. tuna fish
4. peanut butter
5. jam
6. Answers will vary.

Page 22
Growing Rice in Asia
Water buffalos are used to plow the rice paddies.

The farmers plant the rice by hand in the flooded paddies.

At harvest time, knives are used to cut the stalks of rice.

Growing Rice in America
Rice is planted by airplanes that drop the seeds.

Water is sent through pipes to flood the fields.

The rice is harvested using a combine, which is a large machine.

Page 72
1. Answers will vary.
2. tessara
3. siete
4. zehn
5. cinq
6. ocho
7. drei
8. deka

Page 73
1. yi
2. ni
3. walo
4. Nau
5. shichi
6. Chey
7. san
8. apat

Page 105
Suggested answers:

The man traded the cow for the magic pot.

The pot danced away and got some food from the greedy rich man's house.

The pot danced away and got some wheat from the greedy rich man's house.

The pot danced away and got the buried gold from the greedy rich man's house.

The pot danced away, took the greedy rich man to the North Pole, and was never seen again.

Page 107
Suggested answers:

The characters in the story were Jack, his mother, a stranger, the giant, and the giant's wife.

The setting of the story was a small cabin and the giant's house in the clouds.

Event 1: Jack traded the family cow for some magic beans.

Event 2: Jack's mother threw the beans out the window, and they grew into a giant beanstalk.

Event 3: Jack took one sack of gold from the giant.

Event 4: Jack took the hen that laid the golden eggs.

Event 5: Jack took the golden harp from the giant.

Event 6: Jack chopped down the beanstalk, and the giant fell to his death.

Page 108
Suggested answers:

The Magic Pot

About a man and his wife

Traded a cow for a magic pot

Pot danced

Pot took from greedy rich man

No danger for the couple

Woman asked pot where it was going each time

First - pot brought food

Second - pot brought wheat

Third - pot brought gold

Fourth - pot took rich greedy man to North Pole

Pot never seen again

Both

Did not have enough money

Met a stranger on the way to town

Traded the cow for something magical

Man's wife and Jack's mother—angry about the trade

Poor people got things from rich person

Got lots of gold

Poor ended up happy and rich

Jack and the Beanstalk

About a widow and her son

Traded a cow for some magic beans

Beans were accidentally planted when thrown out window

Jack climbed beanstalk

Jack took from rich giant

Dangerous for Jack at giant's house

First - Jack took sack of gold

Second - Jack took hen that lays golden eggs

Third - Jack took golden harp

Giant chased Jack

Jack chopped down beanstalk and giant was killed